Memories and Pain

→ MICHAEL OLLERICH ←

WESTBOW
PRESS®
A DIVISION OF THOMAS NELSON
& ZONDERVAN

WestBow Press books may be ordered through booksellers or by contacting:

WestBow Press
A Division of Thomas Nelson & Zondervan
1663 Liberty Drive
Bloomington, IN 47403
www.westbowpress.com
844-714-3454

ISBN: 978-1-6642-7188-3 (sc)
ISBN: 978-1-6642-7190-6 (hc)
ISBN: 978-1-6642-7189-0 (e)

Library of Congress Control Number: 2022912702

Print information available on the last page.

WestBow Press rev. date: 08/25/2022

BOOK DEDICATION

This book can only be dedicated to the one person who changed my life for all time. My life has been dangerous painful and cruel from a young boy until I escaped to the army. The person who saved me was my wife, Sheila, who would show me that I was not a bad person. No one will ever know as I do, how intelligent Sheila was. When she went to the university in New Mexico, the professors told me that when Sheila took a test her grade was always above 95% and the other students might have the next highest grade of 47%. So, you see we cannot include her in the curve, or everyone would fail.

After we met it was like she knew everything about me even though I never told her much. One night we were watching TV and she looked at me and said your childhood was dangerous and you were hurt. I looked at her and ask how do you know this? She said when we sit here you will just fade away and you cannot hear me. In a normal voice it takes 5 minutes or more to bring you back. She said can you talk about it. I got all flushed and I was terrorized and said no I cannot do it not yet.

Sheila knew that I was a good manager and should have my own company. I liked engineering or I lived engineering. She saw me start with three employees at a company when I first started. Within eight years I would have nine offices and 200 employees. The main office was a corporation where everybody worries about making the boss happy instead of doing their job.

Sheila started our company and controlled the company for as long as she was alive. We had 45 years and then she was gone, life is short. That has been seven years ago already. I sit alone and think of the happy marriage, the children, then her big dream of grandchildren. She did get to meet of few of the grandchildren, but her life ended. Thank you Sheila for giving me everything and I will see you in HEAVEN.

Memories and lesson of long ago

As I get older, I can finally talk of **some** of my past. So, what should I do when many had listened to me and could not believe how dangerous and painful many things were to my sister, brothers, and me? Finally, I have decided to try and write them. The memories were painful but now can be written, maybe I had stopped 2 hours after I started because of the pain flooding in. My sister Mary asked me if I had come to terms with my past and I said yes, but the more I recall I have not come to terms with any of my shattered life. Now 10 months into my project, I have only made notes and a few lines (I do not know if I can do this).

The more I study myself just writing is not the real story. The more I do on this project the more I must tell what happened. What I learned may change your life. For most of my life I could see good and evil sort of like black and white and I kept asking myself, what is the meaning. Yes, the killer is bad but if you do not kill or do anything like that are you still good? This question almost drove me up a wall. What I was asking myself could not be defined. So I decided to look at it in a different way. I should look at actions and then determine if they were evil or good.

Before I was in first grade, I had a favorite place to go. My older Sister Mary took me across the highway and up the trail where the grass and alfalfa was growing and smelled good. The field was one section or 640 acres and all of it was in soil bank. A soil bank is where the government pays the farmer to let the land lay idle and where health of the land is improved. There were beautiful flowers everywhere from sunflowers, alfalfa blossoms, and all kinds of other plants and blossoms. The next thing that made it so beautiful was the birds. There were all kinds of birds from sparrows to blackbirds to pheasants and quail and many others. After finding the path with my sister, I started to go down the lane almost every day. Since I was not in school, I could spend hours walking and finding different things to look at. It was absolutely my favorite place. During the day, my mother would be busy, and I would slip away for 3 or 4 hours almost daily. Sometimes, I would find ducks and geese in the slough which was about a mile from my house. I loved it so much that I often had a dream about it.

After being abused many times the pain stopped, and I was walking down my trail with the son warm on my face and the cool breeze coming at me. The birds were all around me. I was happy it was such a beautiful day and I just kept walking all the way to the sloughs to see all the big birds swimming and splashing. Suddenly, I could hear a voice that said can you see me. It was my big Sister Mary who had come home from school. I could not figure out where the whole afternoon went.

I knew they were going to beat me and take my shirt and pants off. But I could not remember what happened, but I remember going for a long walk, but I do not know if I had gone for a walk. I was happy that I did not remember getting hit or the worst part being nude and getting slapped on my butt or back and being rubbed so hard the pain would almost make me pass out. I knew the people that would abuse me and after a few minutes with them I always ended up walking on my favorite path. Each time I went down my path, I would be happy. When the other kids came from school, I would run to them and hug one of my sisters. I knew I was safe.

When I finally got to fourth grade the sexual assaults stopped but the physical abuse continued. When the physical abuse started and got bad, I would end up on my walk to the big trees and big cottonwood trees. As time went on, I would go on my path and have a good time. The pain would send me away to a world of no pain and after time I would come back from my walk and my sister would be there and I had no memory of what happened, but I would be bruised and cut but no memory. As time went on, I went to my place with no abuse.

I was in first grade when I saw other kids playing some were genuinely nice and some mean. I would ask myself I guess some people are mean but what does that mean. I asked this question for years. Finally,in my junior year the answer came to me. I must write down every behavior. I must look at this behavior and decide is that good or is it evil. I finally had answers for the boys who hurt the child with polio. They were not mean because that does not have a meaning. No, they are evil as evil as Satan. You must look at every action and decide what evil is. Start by defining good. For example, a child must be nurtured by teaching them about spiritual meanings, reading and writing, family values and how to act around other people. In other words, it is your responsibility to see that the child grows in knowledge, love and all the good attributes are learned. To yell and scream, take drugs and alcohol in front of the child is evil. Say the word and define the word and actions.

When you see an adult slap, a child means the person hitting is ignorant and evil. I was in a store 20 years ago and I heard a slap, a hard slap and I turned around. The mother had back handed an eight-year-old beautiful little girl. I dropped what was in my hands and walks straight for the child. I got on my knees and held her to control her sobbing. As I held the little girl she started to calm down. The mother yelled at me to get away. I told her in a low voice you have just assaulted a child and the police are going to take you away because I will press charges. I have never raised my voice because that would upset people and to me is evil. After a few minutes, the child was getting better, so I stood up and asked the mother why. She said the little girl did not listen. I said why is it that my children were never hit and always within reason listened to my command.

I looked at her and said what you did is evil. Before yelling and hitting you must take a breath relax and know that if you think about what you want before you do anything. Then start by talking to the child in a quiet voice and tell your desires. If the child is young and wants to run just say stop. They will stop and then explain to them why they should not run because someone might get hurt. Look at your own lives how evil are you?

To give you an example, we must define the child. If I do something to a child did my action improve the child by increasing spirituality, education, family, safety, and is the child better off because of my action. Anything that does not fit into the improvement of the child is evil. For example, day after day older kids would call me fat boy. Hay fat boy work harder. Hey fat boy how was your day. This is evil. Your mother tells you that you better get your grades up or you will be like the other kids. This mother is evil. Help the child to improve grades or be quiet. Look around you and define every action of yourself and the people around you. Not all the actions but each individual statement or action. There are two basic reactions from any statement. If the child says 10 years old is acting up do you yell and scream, or do you simply say please what you are doing is not nice. We must go to the car, and we will go home so you can have nap and get over what is causing you to act up.

Over my many years, I hear adults say I cannot control that kid unless I hit him. This is very ignorant and evil. He is probably acting up for you because this is the only way you show him any attention. OK I might have tapped a kid on the butt, but he had no pain or anything from it. What I usually do is say what is wrong; there must be something wrong for you to be that upset. This form is constructive and good. I have had a child act up, but I did not hit instead tell them to calm down so we could talk. By my definitions,my friends had mostly evil parents and siblings. At my age I can look back and it becomes crystal clear who was evil and who was not.

When I was in seventh grade, we had two boys that were freshman's who thought that hurting an eighth-grade boy with polio was funny. The second time I saw these two boys knock the polio victim down I lost it. The child with polio wore braces to support himself. Also, this child was extremely poor. And some of my classmates would laugh along with the older boys. I ran towards the evil kids and started punching until the teacher pulled me off and the two boys were bloodied. Of course, the teacher sent me to the principal's office. The two boys that were bleeding were taken to the nurse where they supposedly told how mean I was because the nurse came and told the principle what I had done. The principle said that I was mean and suspended from school for two weeks. I said can I tell my side and they said no. So, I simply walked a few miles home.

When I got home my dad said did you quit, just joking around because he could see how mad I was. He told me to just calm down and we would talk. An evil person would have said what did you do? What kind of person are you? After a few minutes I explained, and my own father said that you have had a rough day but tomorrow I will take you to school.

My dad walked into the principle and said my son is going to tell his side of the problem in this school. The principle said he did not have time and my own father stared at him and said sit down now. My father said Mike take that chair and I will sit here. The principle started to talk, and my own father again stared at him and told to be quit. He looked at the principle and asks if Mike could tell his side of the problem. I think the principle did not know if he should talk. But then said what is your side. After telling my story my father looked at him and said you cannot be this indifferent to a boy with polio unless you do not care for children. My father told him now, what are you going to do? He said let me think about it for a while and I will get back to you.

My father looked at him and said you cannot be this ignorant. The mean boy's father was president of the school board, so he could do no wrong. Finally, after setting there in silence for 2 minutes, he finally said I made a mistake Mike you did nothing wrong because teachers are in the schoolyard to stop this behavior. I started to talk, and he is said be quiet to me. My father looked at him hit his fist on the table and said you are that indifferent to logic.

My dad looked at me and said do you have anything to say. I said yes, I do. Go ahead and tell what is on your mind. I told them most of the teachers would go off by themselves and talk and smoke. My father thought for a minute and said are the teachers not concerned about the safety of the children. I stated they are not. My own father said it is time to get rid of about half of these teachers and find real teachers. So, I did not get off from school for two weeks but had to go back to school and the other evil boys sent home. The evil ones quit school in their sophomore year.

How bad was my grade school? My friend and I taught math and physics in the seventh and eighth grade because the instructor could not figure algebra out or simple physical formula for a cannon ball. The typical examples were given in the book and the teacher could not do it.

How do you start to tell everybody about your life experiences? I guess we should start at the beginning. The first I remember my family we were living on a farm. The house was heated with corn cobs and rarely with coal in the furnace located in the basement.The heat came up by gravity with one register in the living room floor.

The house had no insulation and was very cold with one floor register located in the living room. There were 2 bedrooms on the second floor which had no heat except what came up the stairs. After a few weeks in the winter, windows would have two inches of ice on the inside of the glass. The house had no running water, nor did it have any plumbing at all. All water was carried in five-gallon buckets from the well a block away. All wastewaters drained into another bucket under the sink and carried out. The bathroom toilet was 75 feet north of the house. At five years old, the bathroom was very cold on your bottom.

Finally, I went to school and in first grade I had the most awesome first grade teacher whose name was Mrs. Dresh. Time continued and I start realizing after school when I got home my dad was gone, some adults were not themselves. They almost changed their personality to be dangerous. The young kids could not understand those behaviors but soon found we needed to have different hiding places. When we ate, I noticed they were being different so we would run to our hiding places of which I had two in the house and one out in the barn. Sometimes we would not get to the hide out and you might get smacked around, hit with a belt or the worst your ears might ring and could hardly walk. I always had a lot of bruises. My brother Jim was one year older than me and my sister, Victoria was two years older than me. We had an alarm they would set so we could hide before we got hurt.

We had an older woman who would come out and baby sit Jim,Victoria, and me. At the time I was seven years old. At first, she was genuinely nice and would read stories to us. Then she wanted to give me a bath and she would hit my bottom hard, take my close off and play with me. She stuck things up me which hurt. She would hurt me until I would scream. Enough of this, I cannot go on about this. Maybe later I can tell you more.

I know she would give baths to Jim and Victoria, but I had to leave the area. Suddenly, I am very tired. Thinking this far back about disgusting humans, I must quit writing. I was tired, and this is too much I am going to hit of bed. During the night I started dreaming about what she had done and much of it hurt me physically bad. In my dream I was choking and could not breathe. Suddenly, in my dream, something smelled of cigarette butts and sweat from a person that had not bathed for weeks. I could see myself on top of the fat old body. I awoke in a sweat that I did not have for many years. This project should never have been started.

A few nights ago, I had a dream about running and hiding. The more I ran the more they started to chase me. Someone could always find me, and I could see more people after me and they could find my other brother and sister. I would scream but nothing came out. I have finally realized if this project continues I will probably loss my mind. Suddenly, I woke and looked at the clock. Since starting this project, I have been waking up most nights with nightmares starting at about three AM. There was no reason that I could think of for waking at this time. Over the past 40 years, I remember having many nightmares. Now that I have started the project, I am dreaming almost every night. I have been on this project for almost 14 months mostly taking notes on what I could remembered. Over the past week I have started writing and it is mostly painful.

Now two more weeks have passed, and I woke up at 3:30 AM. The dream I had was someone beating me, and I had my close off. The memories started filling my mind. After all these years and working on this project and why now do memories come to me. I have not had this abuse for many years. Now I remembered as if it was yesterday. It was the middle of the night, and someone came up and pulled me out of bed. It was hard to wake up, but I could feel my night shirt coming off.

At first, I thought it must be bath time. I tried to turn over and then I felt her belly area and it was incredibly warm. Currently, I think I was five years old. I started to get cold and turned to her and now my belly was on hers and it was warm. Now she put me between her legs firmly around me and squeezed me hard. Then the pain increased, and I started down my path and wanted to see the big trees. That was the last time I ever tried or felt the urge to cry or show any emotion. It was time to be a big person and let the person hurt me because they want to, and I could do nothing but take it. I woke in the morning alone in bed.

At this point I must say that the people that hurt me were not my family. The persons that hurt me are all dead and not related to me. Even if you knew me you would not know the person that abused me.

These thoughts started and I realized this had happened many nights and the pain were pushed out of my mind and when it started and until it was over, I get strong enough to block everything. This made me happy because whenever and whatever they did I was strong, and I had felt nothing. In fact, even now I do not feel much when I see even a car accident and people are bleeding and I say that is terrible, but I would feel nothing. I should not have started this project.

All my life I have had pain but now after opening my memories and seeing all the pain is more than I can take. I know now that long ago I did not cry from my eyes, but my heart was torn apart. Why am I reliving my past and why does it hurt so deeply? My Sister Mary told me that someday I would be strong enough to confront my past. I know my Sister, Mary went through terrible times and she had been strong enough to confront her past and look at all the demons in her past. I could see in her eyes when she talked about progress of looking at her past. Many times, she would tell me not specifics but the anguish, terror, and fight to get through it.

Finally, memories are really coming back, and **they are beyond belief**. I cannot believe I started this project. I am going to stop this madness. Put it on a removable drive and put it in a drawer. Stop!! I can do this, and no way will I quit. I wish I would have left everything in the past. I have tried all my life to help people that were being bullied. I have tried to be a particularly good person and help people. All the time I could help but now I must stop this mad project.

Well, I got my disk out and loaded it back on that computer. I could not do anything on my project for more than a month, but it kept telling me that I should finish this, and I will be a better person no a stronger healthier person.

After going through the abuse by adults I know now what evil is. It is everywhere. I think everybody including myself can be evil. Anyone who hits the child is evil no matter what they have done. I have always had control of any child where I am, and never would I hit them because that meant I am out of control and not smart enough to take control of a little kid. When you have a person bigger than you and he is out of control do you hit them? Why then do you hit the little kids. If you did hit that person, you would probably lose your teeth. So, what do you do? You start talking to them and get them too slow down and talk to you. Why? You hit the little kid but now you must think and act like an intelligent person. If you had been slapped hard by a big person you become afraid, and that person slips from your life because when you see them all you feel his pain and no love. Even once you may damage your relationship with a child that will not come back. To the child you are not love you are pain, and you are evil.

I must change my thoughts and tell more fun things in my life. I was about seven when I got my first BB gun. My brothers Jim and Bill had bb guns. At first, we would sneak around and try to shoot a sparrow or a blackbird. After some time, we started to hit them with BBs, but the guns were not strong enough to hurt them. The BBs just fell off them and they all flew away.

The second year we had our guns, we decided to start a war and so we put on welding goggles to protect our eyes. Our first time at war came and I was thrilled. I snuck around hiding in different places sometimes I would get a quick look at Jim trying to get me. I had seen pictures of army guys hiding, so I decided to go by the hay and cover myself up and wait. After what felt like hours which were only a few minutes I had my sights on him. I squeeze the trigger and hit him in the belly. We made sure never to shoot for the face area. We could not shoot more than a foot from a belt line. Of course, he hit the ground and pretended to be shot.

I never had fun like this before. We always had a jacket and strong pants on, so the bbs never hurt. About a month into the war games that would change. I saw my brother only about 10 feet from me and he had me in his sights. I knew I would never get away because I was careless and did not follow the strong standards for evasive actions and hiding maneuvers. By now if you did not follow strict rules, you would be shot. Anyway, I saw the gun barrel pointer at may, and I tried to dive to the ground and roll but it was too late the bullet OK BB hit me in the knuckle and stuck. It did not feel good, and I was bleeding. My brother said first blood buddy and we both started laughing. The second year we did this war game we continued to hide better, and it was becoming difficult to find the enemy. Anyone could say stop and we would put our guns down.

Now in our third year we would start more than 200 yards apart on the home place and one would yell go. We would use what I learned later in the army was flanking positions to get close the enemy. After a few months it was not fun anymore because we could hide and move clear across the farm and neither one of us could find the other. So, after more than three years we quit the war game but later I would learn how much we had learned about evasion.

The first six months in Germany I found out that the army would have war game just as I had done has a kid. Everybody including the German people, German police, German MPs, and infantry that had done this before would all be somewhere to capture you. There was a city we had to go to be safe. Of course, once in the city limits you were safe. I studied the Topo maps and determined the way I would travel to make it. I memorized every creek bridge hills towns and anything that would guide me the 40 miles. Once dropped off we would have three days and 3 nights to get to our objective starting at 8:00 AM. We were told there was nobody looking for us in the first 2 miles. After being dropped off I decided I had plenty of time and could make it in a long day.

I have walked about a mile deeper into the forest than I had planned. The group dropped off was about 40 MP army guys. In those 10 years that the army had done this no one had ever made it. In fact, the closest person to making it was caught 2 miles from our objective. As I thought of my situation, I knew that after midnight no one would be there to catch me except maybe German police and German MPs. I knew their routine of the army and that if I moved between 5:30 AM and seven the army would be eating. I knew that time for the noon and supper meals and a lot of them had worked to do so they would not be on the hunt. I knew almost everyone would move with vehicles and search maybe 100 yards from the roads. The path I chose was the most difficult in vertical climb. It is good to know how lazy people are. After walking my first 5 miles I took a nap for five hours. I knew that as time went on, the time to catch you would be shrinking towards the objective town.

I woke up, had one cracker and a small piece of cheese, and wash it down with water. I looked to my left, in front, and to the right. I could see the map in my head unfold and I knew where I was. Slowly I climbed a mountain which was exceedingly difficult. This exercise took place in the Icorn mountain area not far from Schwäbische Hall. I knew without a doubt no one would climb this area to catch anyone. So, I acted like it was a walk in the park.

Based on the map I knew I was 6 miles down the road and 34 miles to go. I came down the mountain found a hiding place had another cracker and cheese and took a nap. I always try to sleep from 3:00pm to 6 PM because everyone is looking for us. I woke up and was getting very hungry, so I took out snickers bars I had smuggled with me. It was better than a steak sandwich. I knew the bag of crackers and 3 ounces of cheese would not cut it. So, I took six candy bars and taped them to my leg.

I would learn later that of the 40 soldiers that started half would be caught in the first 24 hours and the first 10 miles of the trip. Over the next 24 hours there were only four of us not captured. Then the start of the third day the rest were caught but since they had gone so far, they were not tortured. Torture consisted of throwing water on you, throwing dirt on you and tying you to a tree. After two hours you were free to go. Real torture did not happen. I was the only one still free but the last 3 caught were not tortured but given a big steak, baked potato, and vegetables with a bottle of good German beer.

On my second day of using the mountains I knew I was within eight miles of my objective. I still had 30 hours to make it and I still had crackers and cheese and three candy bars. I did not know how many were still out there and trying to get to their objective. Nearing the end of the second day I later learned everybody thought I went the wrong way and must have lost my compass. It was put over the radio on the third day to look out for a soldier that had to be lost somewhere. Because some soldiers were caught near the end of the second day, they expected me to be with them. The worst thing you can do is move in a group.

The first few hours when I started, I had two guys follow me, so I hid in rocks and let them pass. For about 3 hours I followed them and kept them about ½ mile ahead of me. I knew if someone were there, they would be captured because they talked in a normal voice that could be heard 50 feet away. Absolutely stupid. My upbringing for three years of hunting each other and years of hunting ducks, geese, pheasant and much more taught me how to evade capture. It gave me power to think I might be first to make it or at least make if the furthest.

What should I do I am only 2 miles from my destination, and I have eight hours to complete my mission? So, I sat down had my last of my crackers and cheese and topped it off with my last snickers bar. Then

I fell asleep and woke at 3 am. I dreamed during my nap time about someone hitting me and coming towards me with a knife and that made me wake up. Why did I wake remembering dreams that were horrifying and someone trying to knife me. Why would I have these dreams?

I knew I had 5 hours to make it less than 1 mile. So, when would people be sleeping and not trying to catch me? The last 1½ miles I had to crawl a lot, but the city streetlights were getting brighter. I told myself you cannot get caught in the last mile. It had rained a lot, so I was thankful I had brought my rain gear, but my legs were wet and cold. It was three days of absolute cold being wet, but I wanted to be the first. The only path I can see from here in this water ditch with 2 feet of water. I slipped through the culverts and started down the ditch and froze! I heard voices coming from a building where guys were hiding to catch me. The only way to get farther would be on my hands and knees in water that was from the mountains and bitter cold. I can see the city sign less than 100 yards and there are more voices and another building with guys looking for me. I then realized how viciously everyone was and they wanted to stop me.

Absolutely no one had ever made it, and nobody was going to make it. I lay in the cold water with my nose peeking out and I had rags around my head. Everybody then walked away from my area, and I could not believe my good fortune. I came out of the ditch inside the city limits and went over leaned against the sign and yelled you lost.

For what I did I was getting three days off which do not mean much because being an MP I could sign out a patrol car and have fun with the German girls. It was unbelievable but every adult my age was fluent in English except if the girl did not want to talk to you.

A few weeks went by, and my partner and I decided to go swimming in what we called MP lake. The reason we called it MP lake was that no one could swim in a lake without a lifeguard. After World War two the military police were the highest authority in a land. The MP could do anything but murder. So, if we were at the lake no person could tell us what we could do. We were the highest legal authority in Germany. We can even throw a German cop in jail. So, we know how much authority we really had. At the lake, friends were down by the shore, and we were talking. I told him I do not care much for German girls because they act more like a servant than a partner. Suddenly,a beautiful girl said we are Americans. The way they acted it was obvious they were Americans.

I went over to this girl, and she said you are a big MP. I am six feet 4 inches and 220 pounds. I said I am a big guy I know. I asked her where she was from? She said you will not know the place. I told her before the army and in high school that I drove semis form both coast and down through Texas, drove toFlorida and many times into Canada. She finally told me that she was from Worthington, Minnesota. I said I was from 50 miles west in Sioux Falls South Dakota and her mouth dropped. We talked the rest of the afternoon and had a ball swimming or hanging around and talking. Years later I met a wife of one of my engineers who had heard about the big MP and the girls from Worthington Minnesota. Apparently, she talked about me in school about the nice huge MP she had met and spent the day with.

I was sitting around and thinking of my third assignment when I was in fort hood, Texas. We got notified that everybody in the first armored division had to take tests. I had no idea what the tests were for so we to the classroom and started taking tests that would last for two days. After two weeks, I was called to battalion headquarters to discuss the test results. Apparently, I am one of their soldiers who got the highest grade of all the soldiers. I ask them what does that mean? Well based on your score you and one other soldier have been accepted into west point. He went on to say that I had two weeks to decide if I wanted to go to west point. I got up from the meeting and could hardly walk because of the surprise. I went back to my unit to decide if I would accept their offer. I always would get out a pad of paper and write at the top pros and cons. After two days I was trying to figure out how to decide if I should go. I decided to go and talk to my Capitan.

When I asked him what I should do, he put his head down thought for a minute and said why do not you talk to someone who has done this and likes being in the army and another one who did the same thing and does not want to in the army. The first major I talked to had been in the army for 12 years and absolutely loved his career. The second person I talked to captain and was out of west point for three years. He started out by saying when I was in your shoes, I had to decide whether I want to be in the army for the next 10 or more years. He said to decide on the next 10 years and being only 19 years old the decision would be extremely hard. He went on to say I just as well make it a career because the war is on, and they will not let you out for at least 12 to 15 years. Based on that you just as well stay in for 20 years. So instead of a 10-year decision that will be your life profession. With that information I stood up and headed for the door when he stated I would have never done it. The next weekend ahead was a three-day pass and headed for Austin, Texas where my Sister Victoria had just moved in with her new husband.

We sat and talked about what I should do. The idea of making a life career was overwhelming. After a nice weekend I headed back to my unit. The other soldier had decided to go to west point knowing that he probably made a 20-year decision on his life. I was called into our battalion commander, and he needed a decision. I knew that after the army I could get a degree and it would be paid for by the army. The commander told me to decide because today was the last day. My decision was that I would not decide my live at 19 years old. With that my decision was final and I headed back to my unit. Most people could not believe that I had turned down west point.

After I had been in Germany for a while, I had realized that I was a greenhorn. I did not know what drugs were, different types of people and how dangerous some people were. I pulled patrol with Everett a 30-year-old motorcycle policeman, from Georgia. When we would get into a situation he would laugh. He said do not decide about anything, because you are probably wrong, and he was right. One afternoon the radio blared and told as two go to an old city where an army truck had missed the corner and hit a guest house building. Upon arrival I immediately start measuring the location of buildings and the vehicles.

After about 20 minutes Everett started to laugh, and the guy would look at me and start laughing again. I could not take it and I went over to him and ask him what is your problem? He simply said look around this situation and look at all the people. I had no idea what he was talking about, so I asked him what I did not see. Finally, he told me he said look at those two guys up on the landing. I said so what. He said those are all gay guys and the two are lovers and they are brothers. I almost hit the floor in amazement. As far as I know those were the first gay men that I had ever seen. Yes, I truly am a greenhorn.

A few days later we were told that a soldier had hurt a young girl. We went to the hotel and preceded up to the seventh floor. We knocked on the door and found two German policemen with a young girl inside. She was setting on the bed. My patrol partner said he had to seem all her bruises and would she take off her panties. After we got the required information, we left the building. Once we are in the patrol car, I said what is going on? He went on to say in Germany prostitution is legal. The governments had a 25% tax. I thought about it, and it made me sick. The idea that young girls would sell their body was approved by the people. The idea of someone's little sister would sell herself and this was condoned by the people. It made my skin crawl to think of all the young people making a living doing this. So that was my visit to legalized prostitution.

Last night I saw on TV some of the dangerous inventions. The one that caught my attention was the machine where you put your feet inside push a button and you could see your feet and toe by the machine continuously x-raying your feet. I remember probably about five years old watching my toes moving around. How could anybody do this without understanding the danger.

When I was first in Germany and pulling patrol, we would stop in at the German police station a few times every night. I always worked nights so the married guys could be home at night. I had finally become a military policeman with a badge. I was immensely proud and wanted to be the best and help the most. At about 2:00 AM my partner Tom and I arrived at the German police headquarters. We heard a commotion in the back interrogation room, so we headed that way. I looked in and there was an American soldier being beaten with a club. I moved fast to the German policemen and grabbed the club from them.

I raised the club and then Tom grabbed my arm to stop me from knocking his brains out. I grabbed a jacket and put it under the soldier's head. The soldier was bleeding bad, so Tom went and called an ambulance. I told everyone not to touch him because we might hurt him more.

After that I walked to the German policemen and pushed him hard into a chair and he flipped over backwards. I told him I should take out my handgun and empty the gun in your head. I ask him why you would do this, and his reply was he is only a black. I grabbed his arm headlock and pulled so hard on his arm his feet barely touched the ground and he was screaming. I threw him into a jail cell and locked the door. I returned to move the other German police and demanded to tell me why he did not stop it. He looked at me and said he is only a black.

I told him he is an American soldier, and you will respect him. At this time, I am so mad I could see stars. I started to walk away but decided that the second German policeman had also broken the laws by not stopping it. Oh, I was furious. I grabbed the second German policemen by his arm and his hair and escorted him into a cell. After an hour I had calmed down, so I called the hospital to see if the American soldier was going to be OK. Three days after this incident I went to the hospital where I learn he had of broken skull. He would be in the hospital for three weeks before he could return to his unit.

When I was still in the police station the German commander came in and demanded that his German policeman should be let go. I shoved him down in a chair and said close your NAZI mouth. He took his hand and slammed on the table. I pulled my club and broke the back of his chair. I did not know yet, but Tom had called for a vehicle to transport the German policeman to the army stockade where they would be imprisoned until a court martial could be convened. After the two bad cops were taken off to jail, I looked at the commander and told him tomorrow afternoon we will meet with every German police officer within 50 miles. Any officer not attending will be fired and can never be rehired. Currently, I had only been a military policeman for two weeks. I would continue to see the soldier at the hospital until he was release. And every time I went there, I ask him to forgive these animals. After I told him I said I cannot believe that I insulted the animal. I finally saw him smile but I could see that any movement was painful.

The German newspaper found out about the story. Any American soldier involved could not speak of the international incident. So, I had people ask me about the incident. She called the newspaper and told how an American soldier was beaten and almost died from the beating from the German police. I looked at the newspaper and here was front page news. After a year in Germany, I knew that the NAZIs were alive and well, they had become the German police. Every time I went to a new area I would stop in and see the police and tell the Germans I almost killed two German policemen for almost killing an American soldier.

About two weeks after the incident, I went to my captain and asked why I could not go on patrol. He said I want to keep you alive. Word is on the street that someone will attempt to kill you. I said that sounds like stuff from a movie and he said you were not the first one, a few years ago we had a military policeman shot down in the streets and thankfully he lived.

I told the captain I will put a hat on with civilian clothes and go out and have a good meal. He told me it was not safe, and our base is not totally secure, so I was restricted to my room, day room and the mess hall. Also, I would be escorted by armed military policeman to the mess hall. I told him that is a little extreme. He looked at me and said any of those guys would have cut your throat 20 years ago and now you think they have changed. Two weeks went by, and the rumor was that I was being shipped to Vietnam. This would make the German police satisfied so that I would not have an attempt on my life.

In the middle of that night, I woke by two people in plain clothes. They handed me an envelope which said secret information on the outside. I assumed it was a cryptology message. I read orders from a commanding general to move to a new unit 78 miles away. The order read that I was not allowed to tell anyone that I was from the military police in Stuttgart. Further all my records would be classified, and no one could see them until they contacted the general's office. I was given a card with information on how to contact the general's office but on the bottom card it stated Michael Ollerich -answers no questions and there was a telephone number to call. I did not even pack my belongings I simply got what I needed for 2 days and was gone.

A few days went by, and a truck pulled up and delivered all my belongings. One of the new MPs asked the driver what he had and where did it come from? The driver looked at him and said that is classified. OK now I am in my new unit and arrived with my MP outfit with the Stuttgart Germany emblem. I grabbed all the cloths and went to the sewing store to have new Frankfurt Germany emblems put on. Later, everybody would ask when I was in Frankfurt because many of them had started there, and I had not even seen a picture. I usually said I did not like the place and did not want to talk about it.

One unit of the military police took care of all field maneuvers, and we were assigned to take care of 3 counties. One day the field MP came to stay with us, and I looked over and that guy was from Stuttgart Germany. I told him we had this thing right now. He started to say how are you and I said quit. I took him in the next room and explained the international incident in Stuttgart, Germany. After that he would never speak of it. I am certain every German policeman looked for me and yes kill me if they had the chance.

After about a week I realized the threat was gone. I would pull patrol because that is what I loved. Our motto was Justus with honor. The honor meant we were to serve the people, respect the people and help the people and jail the bad guys. Every day we would escort a shipment of money from our post to another post where the money was locked in the vault. The people caring money where the bank tellers and they were young beautiful German girls. I hated that trip which was made in the morning and every night. So other MPs liked the trip so they could get to know the girls in fact one on my friends married a tall German teller.

After I was there a few months, bank robbers killed two military policemen in Darmstadt. We were devastated. The bank robbers went inside the bank and before they had done anything no one knew they were even going to rob the bank these two policemen walked by the front of the bank and were shot with 12-gauge shotgun to their chests. The front gate heard the guns and sounded an alarm closed the gate and loaded his automatic M 14 rifle with armor piercing rounds. When the robbers left the bank, they were fired on them by the gate guard which caused them to dive under a car.

Any type of action against the army will have contingency plans to control the situation. The artillery unit which had two armored personnel carriers loaded with ammunition and 50 caliber guns were activated. All military personnel tuned their radio to the emergency channel and immediately soldiers knew the situation. We thought the robbers were German national, so we contacted the German police. The gate guard fired a few rounders to hold the robbers in place. The MPS pulled their automatic weapons out of their trunks and started to surround the area. By now the robbers knew there was no way out.

The robbers would be extremely dangerous because they had already killed and would stop at nothing to escape. Think about it, go to the most heavily fortified place on earth and you are going to steal their money unbelievable!!!! The German police arrived on the scene, and we had talked to the robbers, but they would not give up. One of the old Nazis German policemen asked if he could use the 50 caliber twin machine guns just to fire a few rounds and scare the guys. Up to this point the military police were in full charge of the situation. When the German policemen ask to borrow equipment, I was not in charge of those vehicles, but the major does control the equipment.

We ask the robbers if we could call for an ambulance. The MPS had worked into the robber's area and were only 150 feet away. One MP called out to the robbers that we would do nothing, but we want an ambulance to pick up the soldiers. After a minute, the robbers yelled back that the medics could come in and get the wounded soldiers. At least the wounded men were in the ambulance. Later, we learn they were dead before they hit the ground.

The major who oversaw the post, German police and I met in the military police headquarters building. They all asked me if I wanted to be in control and make all the decisions. I thought for a minute and told them if I get up on that 50-caliber machine gun I will fire until all the bullets are gone. I looked at the German policemen and said these robbers are probably German and for that reason I would recommend that one of your man who knows how to fire the big gun send a few rounds in their direction to see if we can stop more carnage. I ask the major if he had any objection. After a few minutes we had a decision that the German police control the scene at least for the time being.

The German police officer got on the radio and ask any of his patrolmen if they knew how to fire the twin 50 caliber machine guns. Within 3 minutes German police came in and stated that he was familiar with the 50-caliber gun. He had been in Vietnam with the first Cav with the Americans. So, we asked him to go to the all-purpose troop carrier which had more than 3 inches of plating.

For about 30 minutes we talked with the two robbers and now we had to call them murderers. We had gotten our telephone from the doctors about our soldiers who were butchered. I got so furious at his word I went to the vehicle with the machine guns but was stopped by two of my MPs. I thought for a minute and decided it would be stupid to get on the machine and kill them. In addition, the damage caused by the machine guns would be unbelievable. The 50-caliber round will break the engine in half and when the bullet would come out of the engine it would not stop but keep going into another car. I thought more about what was going on and was happy that I would not be shooting the big guns because if he shoots the gun 10 times it will destroy 10 cars.

The German police officer got into the all-purpose carrier and jacked a round into each gun. The head of the German police went into the vehicle and whispered something to the officer that would be shooting the big guns. The final warning was given to the robbers to drop their weapons and come out. One of the big rifles fired one shot and part of the engine flew out the engine hood of a new Mercedes. Well, I thought one car down and many more to go. The men shooting the 50-call looked at his superior and the superior nodded his head. The robbers were in behind the third row of cars when the big guns opened fire. The shooter pulled both triggers starting 10' left of the robbers and when he quit, he was firing 24' to his right. Also the shooter was moving the guns up and down.

Finally, the guns were silent. We decided to count rounds fired. Each gun had fired 450 bullets that weighed 1 ounce and traveling at more than ½ mile per second. The robbers were dead. In fact, it was hard to find a body part bigger than their feet. A total of 27 cars were totaled because the bullet did not stop after going through the car but continued through more than four cars. The military police had cleared the area for 100 yards across the base in the area that the bullets would be fired.

After the bullets stopped everybody just walk away and sat down to get their adrenaline slowed down. I sat on one of the rocks by the gate guard area when the soldier who fired the gun came over and sat by me. I told him that I cannot believe why the robbers would not put their guns down and give up. Germany does not have the death penalty. He looked up at me and said Oh yes, we do. I said no legal way to kill a murderer I have read a lot of your laws and then has been stricken down. Again, he looked at me and said go to the newspapers and looked up every person that kills and see how many were apprehended. If the German police know for certain that a person has committed murder, they will all be shot before they are captured. I will do my research and let him know because I saw him around town many times. A few days later I went to the newspaper office and researched eight different big city newspapers and out of many people charged with murder were killed on site. Not one person that murdered were caught and brought to justice. So much for the states who do not want capital murder.

For the next two months nothing really happened. I completed my 12-hour workday and always the night. Working nights were particularly good. Except for weekend nights nothing happened after 11:00 PM so we all would sleep until 7:00 AM and then we would get off duty and have fun.

Last week, Tom and I went to the oldest walled city in Germany. It was the same place we were at when the movie chitty chitty bang bang was being filmed. When we heard that the city would be made famous by the new movie, we took a patrol car with Tom and drove up to see if Dick Van Dyke were onsite. It was funny as we approached the city there was a roadblock. No one was there but the sign read stay out. This time the sign extended across the road. I stopped my car got out and kicked the sign into the ditch. I got back into the car and Tom was laughing uncontrollably.

I looked at him while I was laughing and told him only if it is in my away. We drove up to the walled city which had a gate guard to stop everyone from entering. As the man walked up to my patrol car I drove in, and Tom started laughing harder. By this time, my cheeks hurt from laughing so hard so hard I pulled the patrol car off the road put the seat back and grabbed my sides. I told Tom laughing is a lot of work. Tom started laughing until he was going to pass out, but he threw the car door open and walked away. I sat there for 15 minutes, and Tom did not come back so I walked over and around the corner to a genuinely nice guest house where Tom was eating a big steak.

We drove around the town and there was the old car that every on would see in the movie. We drove around more streets and there was the full cast, and they were shooting the movie. We stopped our car and sit down on the engine hood. A man ran over and said you cannot be here. I ask him are you ignorant. He got read in the face and said aren't you going to leave? I looked at him and said do you want to go to jail? Again, Tom and I started laughing. The man said who are you? Tom told him when it comes to justice this person is the big man. All the cameras were turned off and they took a break hoping that we would go away. Finally, we got in our car and headed back to our police station.

The criminal investigation department was always looking for a patrolman that would go to the big cities and go undercover. Tom was asked to go undercover and Darmstadt who had a big drug problem. The drug of choice was Mescaline which was a derivative of L S D or can be obtained in the mescal buttons from the peyote cactus. Only two days has passed, and Tom had decided to go undercover. I told him why would you do this? He said I can grow my hair long look terrible and maybe make some money on the side. I told him if anybody recognizes you, you are our dead. He laughed at me and said it will not be that dangerous. So, the next day Tom and I headed for narcotics and drug school. The instructor started with marijuana and when he burned a small amount, I could not believe my nose. I have been smiling that odder in our day room and most of the bars in our town.

Only the second week after school I got a call from the hospital Tom had been stabbed four times. My heart sank and I ask will he make it and they said we do not know. Tom had been at the train station and the northern city and was attempting to buy a large quantity of drugs. Tom was carrying 30,000 dollars on him when someone recognized Tom as a military police officer. Later the man was caught who had recognized him and stabbed him.

When we were in Germany or any other country and undercover, we could not carry a weapon. I always carried a snob nose 357 caliber handgun that would blow your arm off. I called the MP station and told them what had happened. I ran fast to get my uniform and badge and jumped in my car and headed 200 miles to the hospital. All the time I drove, all I could think of being stabbed four times in the chest area. There is no way anybody could live through that. Later I would learn that when they caught Tom, he started yelling they are going to kill me. Only a few minutes after being stabbed the German policeman found Tom in a pool of blood. One of the German policemen had been a medic in the German army. After calling the ambulance the German policemen took a long strip of cloth from Tom's jacket and bound him extremely tight. The good part if there is one it was only 9 minutes from being stabbed and being on the operating table.

I arrived at the hospital and ran inside to find my best friend dying. I just had to stop writing because I am crying for the first time in 67 years.

Well 4 days have passed, and I can probably continue my project. On the fifth day Tom looked at me and gave a small weak smile. It would be a close call because Tom had been unconscious, and his heart stopped three times. The army called an emergency meeting because Tom has a rare blood type. At the beginning they could not get enough blood and resorted to plasma or something like that. On the third day the doctors had no more blood because they had filled his body four times. The four men that had stabbed and almost killed Tom were caught in a house and executed by the German police. Well, they resisted so we had to shoot them 14 times.

After the hospital Tom could not even walk. I brought him home in my car and he said I will never do that again. To do that is nothing more than suicide. A month later a bulletin came out that an undercover military policeman was murdered. After two-weeks Tom could shuffle his feet if he had his crutches. At three weeks I went down to his room and told him get your crutches and I will take you on patrol. His spirits rose and for the first time he started to laugh. After two hours, he said I must go back I need a nap. For me this was a great start. After one more month Tom went back on patrol with me.

I have never taken drugs unless they are required by a doctor. In that time, I watch military policeman and other soldiers change after using marijuana. The people I observed lost IQ and any drive to be good. In fact, the ones who used marijuana three times a day, or more could not function and were a liability and a danger to everyone. Two patrolman used marijuana 2 times per day. Both were removed from the MPs. Both went back and lost their rank and ended up a private with dishonorable discharges. So, you think that drugs are OK, stop lying to yourselves.

My patrol ended at 930 AM so I headed downtown to get some sleep at my friend's apartment. Before taking a nap, I had a big breakfast, felt lazy, and got into some clean warm sheet. You know some days the bed feels like a touch of heaven. I just laid there and enjoyed the bed. I drifted off for probably two hours when of blaring speaker woke me. At first but could not understand what they were saying. The patrol knew I was in this area but did not know which building. So, they put on the loudspeaker and drove slowly down the street yelling MIKE come outside we need you. I cannot believe how load that speaker was. I put the pillow over my head and prayed the speaker would leave. But the speaker kept saying, come out

MIKE. Then the speaker said emergency now. I grabbed my shirt socks and shoes with my pants on already I ran out the door.

Since I was the head MP sergeant, I told the patrol this better be serious. One patrolman started to say that they had a 19-year-old soldier who received a dear john letter and was going to commit suicide. I said you can handle this. I said in a gruff voice take me back. They stated you do not understand the person climbed the tower and is more than 400 feet in the air. I said that I had been trained in high climbing conditions but was anyone other than me qualified. We contacted the police station and contacted all the military police and even the German police to see if anybody was qualified to climb with me. Extracting a person from 400 feet would be extremely dangerous and difficult.

One patrol had already picked up my climbing gear which has enough harnesses for two people. After 20 minutes we arrived at the site and found out that no one had ever climbed so I did not have a volunteer. Tom would help me, but he was too weak and could not get half the way up. By now we had 12 military policeman and eight German policemen, and I ask for any one with the ability and training to climb. Everyone as I looked around said no.

When I was eight years old, we had a transmission towers built on our farm. At nine years old I had climbed to the 80-foot level and was having an absolute blast. We did not start at 80 but each time we went back to the towers we would climb a few feet higher and higher until we could climb to the top of the towers or the 80 feet level. No one ever start of the top, but you practice and makes small gains until you lose your fear but never lose your respect or you are dead.

I decided to take my climbing gear and do it alone. I started to climb fast so I was using the two-step climbing technique. The two step is dangerous because if your hands slipped you would fall. My way to climb would be to have one hand on a rung and one foot on the rung. The safest way would be to always have three points on the latter with only one hand or one foot going up. When I was at 50 feet high, I noticed a winch cable which ran from the ground to the tower top and back down. I stopped and went back down. Everybody said what are you doing and then I showed them the winch cable. I tied the cable to my harness and the other end to a jeep. I started to climb on the inside of the tower and said pull harder with the jeep. I let go of the latter and the jeep pulled me to the top. If not for the jeep and winch I would never been able to bring the man down. Absolutely impossible for one man. Now I was talking to the man and put a harness on him. Once I had him tide off, I could finally relax.

I talked to the man for a few minutes and told him that he was totally safe. Then I attached him to the cable and said we will be fine? The cable was strong enough to pick up two jeeps. I continued to talk to him, but he would not let go. For more than ½ hour I tried to convince them everything was OK. Finally, I told him to grab the cable with one hand and as soon as he did that, I hit his arm and other hand and finally he was just hanging from a cable. Slowly the jeep backed up and lowered him to the ground. Then it was my turn, and I attached the cable and let go. Finally, we were on the ground. Thinking back, we would have never saved him without the cable winch.

My son Ryan and I were sitting in the Denver Airport when he was about 12 years old. We are waiting for a plane to take us to Arizona. I picked up a newspaper and on the third page it stated that all nuclear defense systems in Germany were not classified anymore. I showed it to my son and told him that I could finally talk about nuclear weapons in Germany. Because of my Clarence I was taken to the vault in the basement of an old German barracks in the safe there were 84 atomic miniature bombs that were shot from an artillery cannon 15 to 20 miles. He showed me maps on the wall that showed army posts every 30 to 50 miles and all contained 20 or 30 nuclear weapons.

I told the sergeant in charge that the president Nixon had lied. He looked at me no, he said the president did not lie because all American post in Germany are on American soil which were confiscated after World War two. I cannot believe that when we are on our post it was no different than the standing in South Dakota. Later, I would go to riot control school in Southern Germany at the most beautiful ski area. Then the sergeant took me into a small room in the safe where there were boxes that were 4 feet long 1 foot wide and two feet high. He uncovered a box looking item and said this is the big boy who is a 10-ton nuclear weapon that will be carried by a vehicle behind Russian Lines set up and be set off if the Russians invade. I could not believe what I saw. In case of war the American army would pull back 100 miles which would leave all the artillery units in place.

If the Russians came within 100 miles of our position, then weapons would be fired. I finally understood why the American military was so confident that no one could invade Germany. True it would be an absolute mess, but everybody involved would be killed or die from radiation poisoning. I thought about this for the next few days and felt very safe and sick that we had come to this. We knew there were many Russian spies in Germany and based on that news there was no way to safely invade Germany. I went back to the vault and studied the cryptology equipment and the documents on how to make sure the weapons would be armed and fired by the artillery. The artillery units would practice with projectiles that looked remarkably like the nuclear shells. The artillery did not know anything that was in the vault. I had an occasion where I ask an artillery soldier what he could do if the Russians invaded. He spoke in great confidence that they had many exploding shells and would stop the Russians. What he had would not even slow them down.

After I was in Germany for 6 months, I decided to go behind the iron curtain to see how people were living. I thought that would be fun because I had never been in any of those countries. Four days later we were told to set up the heliport from someone coming in. The post had the grass area which was defended with fully automatic weapons when anybody flew into our post. I met a major who requested to see sergeant Ollerich. I told him that he was looking for me. He said I would go to the military police headquarters so that we can have a talk.

He started by asking me if I had put in for two weeks of leave to travel to the Czech Republic. I told him that the mountains were beautiful and that the people really liked Americans. He looked at me very seriously and said I cannot stop you, but do you realized you have a high clearance and are only five people with cryptology knowledge. We believe that if you cross into the iron curtain you will not come back. The newspaper will tell that you lost control of your car and plunged into a river far below. I ask him does anybody really know that I have a crypto background and an extremely high clearance. He said I think back to eight days ago, when you were pulling patrol late at night and you thought that a drunk almost hit you. And then a fast car took after the apparent drunk driver. I said of course I remember, and I hope that they would catch that drunk driver. Close your eyes and imagine what happened. I setup in amazement. The undercover American soldiers prevented someone from killing me. All the time you have been in Germany we have had people protecting you. We did not tell you this because it is harder to protect you when you are trying to protect yourself.

Remember back to when there was a man with an older Mercedes Benz with his engine hood open. Did you see the man in the back seat? I said no. Well, there was and he had of sniper rifle pointed at the driver in another car who had you under surveillance. I set back in my chair and felt sick to my stomach. I stood up and told him to give me a few minutes and I walked out of the police station. Our conversation had really upset my world. I could not believe what I was hearing. I started to think how many American soldiers were murdered and they were made to look like an accident. I guess we will never know. I could not settle down but went back to the office and told the agent how I felt.

I put my face into my hands and started to shake. The world had always been straightforward and logical and now there are Russians, others spy, murderers and whatever. My world was absolutely shattered. The agent stood up touched my shoulder and said take a few minutes, you deserve it. We talked on for more than an hour. He said because of my Clarence and knowledge of the nuclear weapons I was in danger of being taken. After that I never went out of my bedroom without a knife in each boot and my snub nosed 357 magnum revolvers. Never again would I feel safe unless I was in my bedroom. I did not settle down for more than one month. The agent was right became paranoid which is not good. I had to accept reality.

I guess I do not understand why the more I probe my memory the more terrible demonic dreams I am having. Again, I do not think I should have started the project. But since I have started, I want to try and finish. I remember going to bed and woke to find someone standing over me. It was so dark I could not see who it was. Then fear gripped me because I could smell sweat and cigarettes. I tried to cover my head, but the person pulled the blankets down. Someone was lifting me out of bed with their arm around and their hand over my mouth. I just froze. When they had me downstairs, they started taking my shirt and bottoms off. I did not do anything but lay on her body. I was so scared by ears started ringing and I started to see flashes of light in my own. I do not know for sure if I passed out. The next thing I remember was that I was back in my bed.

About this time my folks had friends who would come over and play cards. They had a daughter my age and she said she really liked me. We played together and it was OK. One day I look out of the window and there they were. I ran to my room got under the bed because I did not want to see anyone. A few minutes past and I pulled back the covers and saw her standing there. So, I got out from under the bed,and we started to play. So as life goes on, I had a girlfriend which I said would never happen. Oh, by the way, I never told anybody.

Well, this project is not going well. No matter when I go to bed I will get up in the middle of that night and it is always 3:00 AM. When I do not wake up, I do not remember dreaming. So tonight, I did have a nightmare. The nightmare started with fog which limited my eyesight making the sounds terrifying. As I walked along by step over a ledge and started falling. There were vines that I grabbed onto and when I look it was someone's arm. The fog was so dense I could not see the persons face. When I tried to get closer, I was thrown down and finally hit the ground. The fall hurts my arms and it to work from the boat for I could get up. Now it if 4:00 AM and I am just looking at the notes I have been taking. I am just looking at the TV that is not on. When I start to remember that I was about nine years old when I was in the corn crib up about 15 feet high when my hands slipped, and my older brother tried to catch my arm but failed and I hit the ground. Wait it was not my brother it was my insane cousin who shoved me off the platform. Only now I realized his name was John. He just laughed and was gone. John was stabbed to death in a bar fight.

When I started to remember the dream about a large person would chase me and he had big knives. I would run but I hardly could move. I would turn around but never see who was after me. This nightmare started incredibly young and once I had the dream it started to come back almost every night. The dream always started with me running and I would try to turn around to see who it was. I could never see who was chasing me, but I knew that if I ran hard enough, I could make it to the front door of the house. No matter what I did I never made it to the front door of the house. This dream would continue for more than four years. After I woke up, I would try to remember what was going on for me to keep having this dream. I knew that the dream would never end until I can figure out what caused the dream. I told some of my brothers and sisters about the dream. They could not explain what happened or why I was having this nightmare.

The nightmares were still coming. I will never forget when I was 8 years old and thinking about my nightmare, I had closed my eyes and then I saw that nightmare unfold in front of me. Whenever we would butcher a cow or hog an old timer with all his knives would come over and shoot the animal. He would then hang the animal in the corn crib and cut the animal apart. While he was doing that one day he looked up and saw me. He said I think I should butcher you and he ran after me. The harder I ran the faster he would run always banging the knives together. He would get close to me and shoved me and would hit me on top of the head with a knife. Finally, the nightmares must be understood what had caused them. What he did was evil, and he was so ignorant he did not even know what he did. I was incredibly happy, that my nightmares stopped after four years of waking up sweating and being terrified. But that was temporary, and it started again.

It seems unreal, but the nightmares are things that really took place. Why do I not remember what happened but first I have a nightmare that opens memories of the past. Something has blocked my memory. Before this project I would tell you that my childhood was a lot of fun and I do not remember anything bad. The more I think about my past the more I am starting to remember the more painful memories come back. It does not make sense why I do not have any memory until I dream or think of about the dream.

I absolutely cannot believe what is happening and I have just got home went and changed my clothes and the batteries in my wheelchair ran out of juice. So, I laid down in bed and fell to sleep. When I awoke, I realized I had been dreaming? The dream started when I was back in the army, and I looked over and there are three boys about seven playing together. They looked at me and waved to have me play with them. I just started to play, and it was a lot of fun. Suddenly, a person's start yelling and stop playing like a dog and yelled get something done and make sure your chores are done. I immediately got up and started and ran.

The house heating was a potbellied stove in the living room. We then got electricity and installed a furnace in the basement. However, every winter we would have to get the old potbellied stove out and use it during the winter storms for at least two weeks. I remember the first phone was the old hand crank. Within a few years we got a regular phone on a party line. People were always listening so my sisters would call their friend and make up stories about people and soon everybody was talking. What they said were all lies but people just kept going on and continued our lies. But most of all I remember how cold the winters were.

I got hurt once and at six years old older brothers and my dad all started laughing at me and called me a baby and started making sounds like a baby. No matter how bad I got hurt from then on, I never tried. In fact, I started to grow through life with no feelings. To this day I might feel bad if a person gets hurt, but I really do not feel anything like are normal person.

When I was in the army, every MP had to see a psychologist who why I do not know. After meeting where them I ask what they had learned. He told me that I had an immigrant personality. Until know, that I did not trust no one and did not feel at home anywhere. Over my Life I said one friend in grade school and the same person in high school. But when we were sophomores, he enlisted into the navy and had a pregnant girlfriend. He had come home on leave and married his sweetheart. They were planning a future in San Diego. About when he was ready to leave, he went in town on his small moped and was struck by a drunk who did not stop for a stop sign. My friend flew over the car and struck his head on the curb. I spent the next 7 days in the hospital when he finally passed on. That was my true friend and never really had one after that.

In the third grade I was working before and after school for 1 to 2 Hours feeding animals shoveling manure for six milk cows, but about 200 hogs confined in a building take a lot of shoveling. Everything we did was Manual labor.

One of the jobs we did was cutting corn and putting it into the silo. A silo is a concrete structure which was about 20 feet in diameter and 40 feet tall. We had a machine that would blow the corn and stocks into the air and down into the silo. I would go to the field with an empty wagon and unhooked the wagon. But I would drive to full wagons, hook the wagon to my tractor and take it to the silo area. At seven years old I felt real pride in my work. In fact, it was extremely dangerous for my age. I would back the tractor and wagon to the machine, start the machine and blow the corn into the silo.

When I was eight years old, I would go into the silo to distribute and pack the corn as we filled silo. When we got to the top of the silo we would fill to the top of the concrete and keep filling until a cone was 10 feet taller than the walls. Looking back this was extremely dangerous. There was a metal ladder inside a metal shaped U where you could climb up and down the silo. The latter would get slimy from the cornstalks. As I started down the ladder my hands and feet slipped. I fell 30 feet down the chute ladder. I rammed a bold into my back and was knocked out. I woke up in the barn when my sister Mary came looking for me. It was dark outside so I must have been in the barn for a few hours. I remember talking but then I passed out. The next thing I remember was waking up in my bedroom. It was insane for me to do this job when I was so young. A few hours later I was very hungry and went downstairs and made a sandwich. The rest of the family did not know I was not around for supper.

That same year I was driving tractor to collect bales from the field. Some people told me to take off my shirt and get a suntan. I did not know better, but I had my shirt off for six or seven hours. By nightfall I had 4-inch diameter blister. I could not work for one week. It was like living in total pain.

By August, the temperature was about 100°F and we were bringing in 8,000 bales. On the fourth day I tried to get out of bed. My legs would not work. I called for my sister Mary to come and help me. After a few minutes I realize that my legs would not work no matter what I did. My two sisters picked me up and took me to the Doctor. I had extreme heat stroke and he said I must go to the hospital. My father said that would cost too much and got instructions from the doctor and we went home. I became delirious and could not see very much. Everything was blurry, I was running a high fever and would pass out. This went on for about one week. My fever finally went down, and my shivering stopped. My legs were working but I could not stand. One week later I could stand on my own but walked very unsteady and weak.

The summer of my 8th year would be a nightmare. A bus came down the highway 77 that was in front of our farm. The bus came to a stop and dropped off a person that looked about 14 years older. He came up to the house talked with my mother. He was a cousin from Iowa. I did not realize how bad that person would be. The first week he seemed OK and spent most of his time with the older kids. Then the pain started. He was hiding in the bushes and tackled me. He started to hit me like he was in a fight. When it was over, both my eyes were swelled up and were black and blue. He simply laughed and walked away.

Being more than twice my weight, I could not believe what he did. I had tried two tell what had happened to older people and they laughed. I hid most of the day unless my brother Bill or Jim was with me. The next day he caught me again knocked me down and took the heel of his boot and jumped on my leg. Again, he laughed and went away. I lay there, tried to get up, but could not. After maybe 1 hour I had crawled into the pickup garage got in and fell asleep. Again, I tried to tell people what was happening, and they did nothing.

My sixth grade I realized that there was the excessive drinking which caused all the dangerous problems. In the seventh grade I was 12 years old. We had moved to a new farm about 7 miles away from our original farm. We still had the livestock on the old farm and my brother Jim, and I got up at 5:00 AM to start working at the new farm and then drive a pickup to the old farm and more chores. After that we would go to school and park the pickup about a block away so we would not get in trouble for driving. After school we went back to the old farm and continued work for another 1½ hour and then continue home in our picked up. Once we got home, we would continue feeding cattle and our hogs until eight or 9:00 PM.

My 12th birthday was great. I did not get any presents from my family, but I got me what I really wanted. I had my older brother buy me a handgun. It was a double action single action western style gun. I also got a fast draw holster. Every day I was outside working I would practice drawing my revolver. I would use the double action to draw and fire the weapon. Most of the time I would do dry fire to save ammunition. After one month, I could draw fast and hit a playing card. I continued during this almost 50 times a day. At the end no one month I was fast. At the end of two months, you could hardly see my hand drawing, firing, and putting the gun in my holster. For safety, I carried my revolver all the time. At night I would go to bed and sleep with my gun. Also, I would move my bed up to block the door from coming open. My brothers believed I just love to play with my gun, but it was for survival. I would make sure that everyone would see me draw fast and hit a playing card with two bullets at 10 yards. He understood I was not fooling around.   After I got my revolver, everyonne stopped harassing everybody.

The farm we moved to be the same farm my father grew up on. My father started to believe that he was back when he was a child. My father started to call my brother Jim by the name of Joe who is my father's brother. In another word my father was having a mental break down. A few months later my father was mad and told my mother he was going to shoot everyone. My father then went to the barn. My sister Victoria called the sheriff. I came into the house and my sister told what was going on. I went and got my shotgun and took it outside. As I went outside, I put the shotgun by a big tree so no one could see it. I knew there was a shotgun in the barn. My father opened the barn door but never came out with a gun. After about 15 minutes, the sheriff drove into the yard. About 20 minutes later, an ambulance drove in the yard. My father came out of the barn with no gun and was taken to and the hospital. He would stay in the hospital for a month.

This was springtime and 600 acres had to be planted. I started by planting the oats followed by corn. I worked from sunrise to sunset for almost one month. I had my brother bring me my schoolwork. At night I would do my homework and send it the next day to the teachers at school. You can see that I never was a child or had anything but work. In grade school and high school, I was never a child but the hired hand with no pay. I only started to make money when I started to drive semis and strait trucks. After I got older, I was very mad because I had no childhood.

About 6:00 PM Richard found out the calves were at our farm. We got of phone call from my brother Bill and said that Richard was on his way with a shotgun. He came driving into our farm and was extremely mad. My sister Victoria had already called the sheriff. Before Richard arrived, I place a shotgun behind a tree. In addition, I had my 6-gun on my side. My father came from the barn and Richard grabbed him and hit him. About that time the sheriff drove in. I was behind the tree with my shotgun loaded and ready to fire. The sheriff told Richard to get off the farmer or go to jail. Richard left the farm.

Uncle Bill (not my brother Bill) and Richard pressed charges against my mother for stealing the cattle. In court my uncle Bill stated that money was owed by my mother to my uncle Bill, and they should have all the cattle. My dad and mother showed that the Bill had been paid to him in full. The judge told my uncle Bill and Richard to get out of the courthouse or be charged with grand larceny.

I drove a strait truck to deliver cattle and hogs from the sale barn as well as feeding 100 cow, 80 yearlings, 90 calves, and 200 pigs. This went on until I was a sophomore in high school. At that time, I have found work with my oldest brother driving semi-trucks to deliver animals sold at stockyards in 6 states.

My brother James at that time came home at night only to sleep and get up early and leave. It was too dangerous for him to be at home and work without some guy to watch his back. I on the other hand did not come from school but went to work at the sale barn and would drive semi-trucks. My older brother Bill was driving a semi to get enough money to go back to college.

At first, I would ride in the semi to keep my book brother from falling asleep. One time he was so tired he could not go on. It would be safer for me to drive and him to sleep. I started driving semis when I was just 14 years old. By the time I was 15 years old I was driving those semis by myself to Canada usually over to Iowa and back to Sioux Falls. Most every weekend during school I would go driving. I would leave Friday night after school and drive to Canada into Iowa. I usually drove 500 miles to Winnipeg Canada some 750 miles into Iowa and be home Sunday afternoon without sleeping. I would go to bed and sleep until Monday noon or Tuesday noon. This meant that I would go to school only three or four days a week. At school I took up all the AP classes and maintain an A or B average. When I was driving, I would bring my books along and read it as I was driving. Believe it or not if you learn to glance up and down this can be completed safely. I continued driving my sophomore junior and senior high school and in the summer of my senior year. I had 51 trips to Canada before I got my driver's license.

While driving to Canada one day I said you were going to die in this truck. I became very scared and needed to figure out what I should do. I had no money because I helped everyone. October 4, 1966, my brother was drafted for the army and then to Vietnam. I immediately went to the army recruiter to see what my future might be. If you join the army for three years you can specify what you want to do in the army if you can pass the tests. I told the recruiter if my brother and I can leave tomorrow, we would go into the army to be a cryptologist. And believe that or not at 1130 pm the same day my brother and I flew out to fort bliss Texas.

Basic training was extremely easy because we had worked all our lives. In fact, I would gain five pounds in our 2 months of basic training. I must tell you that to try and hurt me, my brother will be vicious. I can give you an example. We were not allowed the first month to have beer. So about one week into basic training my brother just stated get dressed we are going out for the night. On the way back, five Mexican men approached us from the front, and one pulled a knife. I told my brother let us go the other way. He said stay here and walked toward the first man with a knife. By this time, he had put on tight leather gloves. As he approached, he stated I am going to put that knife in your stomach. He faked a punch with his left hand and with his right he hit the man with his right fist and the man was knocked unconscious. He picked up the knife and broke the blade off. He walked towards the next man and pretended to strike width his left fist but then did an uppercut to his jaw lifting the man more than a foot off the ground. This man was unconscious. He picked up the second knife and broke the blade off. The other three men ran off.

A few days later we were loaded into a truck and taken to the field for training. On the third day the company commander through a tear gas grenade into our unit. I was on the side and simply walked off. My brother was in the center and the tear gas went off 10 feet in front of him. He put his gas mask on, but it was too late, and the gas was in his eyes and lungs. That night I ask him what he was going to do. He just stated why I would do nothing. About 9:00 we went to bed and soon fell to sleep.

I woke up at 3:00 AM and my brother was just going to bed. I said where have you been? He stated I just went to the bathroom. We then heard a lot of screaming and yelling. After a few minutes we just went to sleep. The next morning, we were told that someone had tied the tent zipper closed in the officer's tent and had to throw a tear gas grenade into the officer's tent. The officers could not get out of their tent. Finally, someone took a knife and cut the tent open. The captain who had thrown the grenade could not unzip his sleeping bag. After another few minutes someone went in and dragged the captain out by his feet. I asked if my brother was the one that threw the grenade into the tent. He said I was sleeping, and I am innocent unless I was sleeping walking.

The captain thought there were possibly two people that would have gassed the captain. And yes, one of the persons suspected of that was my brother Jim. Over the next three days everything went good except that captain was picking on Jim. The captain gave extra work and extra hours for the next three days. Finally, we got our orders to complete our final forced march. This forced march will extend 25 miles. On this march you must have 40 pounds of ammo, wherever you want to eat plus 1 gallon of water and a canteen. If you forget something, you will go without. Well 4 miles into the march, we were ordered to take 30 minutes for a break and get something to eat. About 1 minute later the captain said who urinated into my canteen. The captain's spit it out. About 1 minute later the captain started yelling and said who urinated in my gallon container. That meant the captain must walk 21 more miles with no water. We watched the captain later and he even threw his food away. I looked at my brother and said any idea who did that and again he looked and said I might have been sleepwalking.

It was amazing; the captain would not even look at my brother. He did no more extra hours or extra work. I believe the captain started to fear my brother. Knowing my brother, I would fear him.

The next two weeks went without anything happening but that would be short lived. My brother and I had been on KP one time. We should not be on KP for 3 more weeks. But my brother by himself was given two days on KP. I asked him what are you going to do. He stated that I will go and have some fun. I said what do you mean? He said I do not have the time to tell you so how I want to see if it works. I said what works? He said I will see you in 14 HRS. He went off to KP duty and I thought what is he planning.

I had a good day, because of all basic training was easy. While I was preparing for hand-to-hand combat training, our instructor had been teaching hand to hand combat training for 12 years. Before that he had been in Vietnam for a total of four years. First thing he did was challenge the class four a fight. And of course, one of the guys from Chicago challenged him back. The instructor through a knife to the soldier. The soldier tried five times to stick him and failed. Every time the soldier got close the instructor would slap him which made him very mad. Finally, the soldier dropped the night of and ran after the instructor. The instructor showed us 20 different ways to get away from the knife and to attack the other person.

By the end of the second day no one could stick the instructor with the knife. He taught us to run fast at the other person and at the last second simply go sideways and chop the other person in the throat. By the end of the week, I could easily kill someone who needed killing. The next area we studied was the use of a bayonet. At the end of two more days there would be amazingly simple to kill with a bayonet. The next phase was to fight with a wood dowel 4 feet long with big cotton balls on the end to reduce injuries. I was the first up and the other guy was as big as me, which is 6 foot 4 inches and 200 pounds. I was somewhat scared. I faked with my left hand and delivered a blow with my right hand with a blast to his head. Even with a helmet, he hit the floor like are rock and the instructor said what are you doing? I said I am defending myself. It took 5 minutes for the guy to wake up. The lieutenant told me that I could not do that anymore, which was fined with me.

The third guy up was my brother. I told the instructor not to let my brother fight that guy even though they were the same size. Both were as big as I was. He told me to sit down and watch them. Again, I said do not let him fight. The instructors said quiet. The fight started and my brother Jim faked with the left hand and did an uppercut with the stick to his lower jaw. The soldier went almost one foot into the air. After hitting the ground, the soldier was unconscious. The instructor said you cannot do this fighting anymore. The instructor looked at me and said I should have listened to you.

A few more weeks went past, and we have finally passed basic training. From fort bliss we were sent to fort Huachuca in Arizona. We would start our education with pole climbing which were 40 feet tall. One thing about the army, I had never been around Mexican, Chinese, or black people. Our first instructor was a black man who could climb the 40' poles in eight steps up the pole and return to the ground in two steps. I had never seen a person that could climb so fast. It appeared extremely dangerous but after doing it the few times it was like walking to him. About 1 hour had passed when one of the students climb to the top of the pole and just sit there. I was in awe and so were many of the other students in. We would learn later that this student had been a pole climber for more than eight years for a pole company. He was ordered to go to the main office where he was given his first strip and became one of the instructors.

After two weeks we were given our final exam, which was to climb the 40' poles, stay there for 2 minutes in return to the ground. Three guys could not get more than 10 feet above the ground and were sent to an infantry unit.

I was never a racist because I did not know what it was. I treated every person as a friend. I did notice some people were very mean to the Mexicans and the Blacks. I would ask them why they were acting so poorly. They never gave an answer. When I was in grade school, I never saw a Mexican, Chinese, and 1 black person. Our grade school was rated so poorly it would not matter if you went to high school or not. My father said once we had gone to our new farm, he would send us to a catholic high school that was only 4 miles away. I was enrolled in all the AP classes and did exceptionally well. But by the end of my freshman year, we did not have enough money to pay for those schools.

My friend, Richard and I talked, and he is said that since he needed a driver to deliver cattle in the local area, I could do that since he owned the sale barn. The spring and summer were spent working five days a week for 6 hours a night driving for the sale barn? At the middle of summer, I started driving the semi with my brother Bill. I had my sister Victoria who was two years older than my brother Jim who were both going to the catholic high school. That meant someone must make money to pay our tuition. The only person making money was me. I started driving to Canada every weekend which meant I could not get to school on Monday. So, I went to a priest and explained I had to work. He agreed and told all the instructors to back off. I still took AP classes which was difficult. I would take my books with me to Canada and study when I was driving. After a few days I could read the book by quickly looking at the book and the road until I felt safe to drive. By doing this and working Wednesday and Thursday night driving a straight truck I could get 50 hours worked per week. I am made enough money to pay for school for the 3 of us and have money left over. Everybody in school though I must really be tough to work that hard.

During my first year I went out for football and made the varsity football. I started as a defense tackle. And at the end of the fourth week, I quit. After school I would go to choir and that would make me about 15 minutes late to football practice. I did not have much fun in my live but genuinely enjoyed our choir. The coach said you must choose between choir and football. I walked off the field never to return. Many times, the coach would ask me if I would come back to play football. By that time, I told him I was working and needed the money.

Anyway, back to advance training. On our third week, my brother and I decided to go to the pub and have a few drinks. At midnight we walked back to our unit. There was a group of the Mexicans who told us to walk in the street. I would tell my brother I did not want to fight and just go. My brother put on his leather glove, and I knew what was coming. The first man walked towards my brother with a knife in his hand. Before I knew it the knife was in his hand and the man hit the ground and collapsed. We were more than a head taller and 60 pounds heavier. The second man approached swinging his knife back and forth. My brother faked with his left hand and kicked him between the legs. The man hit the ground and was in much pain. At this time, the rest of the men ran away.

We both were in the top 10% and we went to our next classes on radio repair. We only had one week on this subject. We had to read and study 4 hours every night to keep up. We both passed in the top 10 percent and moved on to our final classes on cryptology. I was glad that we had signed up for cryptology which meant in case of war we would be with the generals in the secure area. The next four weeks we had to study 5 hours every night to keep up. My brother and I were top in the class. Everybody in this cryptology school went to Vietnam except my brother and I went to Germany. He was attached to an artillery unit, and I was attached to the military police.

I arrived at my MP unit and found a vault which contained the machines used in cryptology. I and the lieutenant colonel were the only ones to have the combination. After three days I had set up all the equipment and was ready for war. I went to the company commander and told him my work was complete and I said I have nothing to do. Could I become a police officer? He said I could ride along but could not give any orders until I had past the MP school test. I asked him if he could give me the test. He is said of course he could make the tests available. I said where I can take the tests. He stated that I could not pass the tests without going to classes. Before this I had read the **BOOK ON MILITARY LAW.**

A few days later, a captain called me and said that tests are ready. So I went to his office and took tests that he said would take eight HRS. I started the tests and in 4 hours I was done. When the test scores came in, I was in the top 3% of students. He looked at me and just stated I cannot believe it. If I had not given you the tests, I would have said you had to be cheating.

And now could be a police officer and be on my own or with a partner. I got to our first line up to see my patrol partner was. No one wanted to go with the animal, so we were put together. That would be a mistake. As soon as we got our patrol car he wanted to go to the bad side of town. At about midnight we went into a bar and were walking about 20 feet inside the bar when the light went out. He grabbed me and shoved me under a table. Maybe 20 or 30 beer glasses were flying at us. We stayed under the table for about 5 minutes when a bright light was turned on outside the bar and the door opened giving us enough light to get back up. The German police had seen the light go off in this bar before, so they carried a huge light on their car. The animal looked and soldiers that did not have a glass and started to knock them down and put cuff on them. I helped him and before we were done, we had 11 men in custody. The soldiers were taken by the German police to jail.

I knew why they called him the animal. When the animal and I went on patrol we always phone something to do. About three months of pulling patrol the expected to get hurt but it did not happen the animal was always there to make sure that I was ok.

Currently I was 19 **years old.** I went to basic training in Ft Hood. Then for advance training in Ft Huachuca Az. Then I was attached to the 1ˢᵗCalvery in Ft Hood Texas. I was running telephone lines to 8 eight-inch guns. On the 3ʳᵈ day I walked by the guns when they fired. I was knocked to the ground. Someone ran over to help me, but I could not hear them. After about a week I could hear some, but my ears would ring all the time. I cannot hear anyone if we are in a group and talking. After a few months I was sent to Germany. My ears ring all the time and I have hearing aids. My hearing ability never came back.

In Germany, I was attached to the 385th MP battalion and spent time in Stuttgart, Crailsheim and Swabbish Hall. Before I went to Crailsheim and Swabbish Hall, I walked into the German police stations back room. I found two German policemen beating up a soldier. The soldier was black but that did not matter he was our American soldier. I immediately told them to stop, and they did not. I pulled my 45 handgun and pointed it at the head of the German police. He would not stop, and I had backhanded him with my 45 that nearly took his head off. My partner and I picked up the soldier and called for an ambulance. When my partner took the gun from the German police, he grabbed his handgun and told the other one to give his gun. At that time, I put my 45 away.

This caused an international incident which was controlled by the army since the war. After world war the military police were given authority over everything in Germany. I mean everything. I was told that I could put any person in handcuffs and bring them to the station for processing.

I was kept on base because I was told the German police were the old Nazis. If they got the chance, they would kill me. After the hearing the German Police were fired. And this was decided by our commander that was head of all jurisdictions in Germany. At that hearing I was told I would go back to the United States for safety. Instead I was sent to Cralsheim Germany. I immediately packed all my things and got into a jeep. On the way out of Stuttgart, the man driving said we are going the wrong way. The jeep driver from Sioux City slowed to about 5 mph and was turning left when a speeding bus (I was told later he was going more than 50 mph.) The bus went over a steep hill and hit us. I was thrown out of the jeep and landed about 70 feet into a ditch. I started to come to, but I could not see. My sight came back to a very blurry state. I then looked up and saw what an ambulance. The ambulance took about ½ hour to get there. I thought the ambulance would find us. The ambulance took us to the hospital.

I learned much later from the police report. I felt people lifting me up. I was carried to the ambulance. I came to a few days later in the hospital. A nurse asked me if I knew where you were. I said it looks like a hospital. She said where and I replied in Sioux Falls SD. She said no Germany. I said why am I here? She said I was in the Army. I said no way. I do not remember anything after that because I passed out. I think I woke the next day or few days later I do not know.

The jeep has tubing at the front of the seat. My legs were black from my knee to the ankle and 4 inches wide. The Doctor came and said my back had many fractures and bulging discs. A few days later I called my unit to come get me. I told the doctor I would go to my unit and be a desk sergeant. By the time I got to my unit the pain was killing me. I went to the base doctor and said what had happened. He looked me over and my legs and back of my legs were all black. He said if you are in that much pain we need to go back to the hospital. I had brought x-rays and other papers with me and gave them to the Doctor. Based on all the damage you might not walk again. The best thing would be a medical discharge and go to a hospital in the states.

Months went by and I got better but I always had extreme pain until I got out of the Army. I could never run or even walk fast. When I got out of the Army, I could walk 50 feet with much pain and then I had to sit down.

I finally could walk and pull patrol. During the time I could not walk I worked on cold cases and settled 6 old cases the first few months. The CID wanted me so they could get recognition, but I said no because I had to sign for another year. Because of the pain and no pain pills I needed out of the army. I did make detective because of this.

I did get better and went to college. In college I got a degree in civil engineering. Working I still had a lot of pain. Then one day brushing my teeth I collapsed on the floor and could not move my legs. The pain was gone for a while. I was taken to the hospital where I was for some time to figure out what to do with my spine. This has been many years and you must now go to the records and see when all my surgeries took place. I had surgeries at Sioux Valley hospital, now Sanford Hospital, McKennan Hospital now Avera Hospital, Specialty Hospital in Sioux Falls and the hospital in Albuquerque, NM.

I have had 11 surgeries on my spine with rods and fusions. I had 2 surgeries on my neck with plates. I needed surgery on my wrist, shoulders, knee, and elbow because of pain. I have had 29 surgeries and four in the past year.

I have gone through pain and surgeries for 50 years. But I would not give up my Army experience. I was head of 18 MPs completed many investigations and got my honorable discharge. You asked how I got in charge of 18 patrolmen when I was only 20 years old. We had a sergeant who drank every day and came to our sleeping quarters and would harass two of those smaller MP's. The third time he came in, and I told him he was relieved of duty because he was intoxicated. There were probably five MPs watching this unfold. He tried to push me away, but I would not move so he hit me in the jaw.

Since he hit me first, I could defend myself. I bloodied his nose and his jaw. Finally two other MPS got on him and held him down. One of the guys got scared ran to the police station. That soldier called the company commander, and he was not in, so they called the battalion commander who was a colonel. The officers sent to us were in a jeep and had to travel 90 miles with canvas walls. It got down to 15° that night and the first sergeant was mad. They listened to me and two other men to figure out what was going on. When we had completed telling the truth they had took our sergeant away that night. In addition, the captain said I was the only one to follow the military code of justice and therefore I would be in charge until he contacted me.

I was told to go to see our company commander and given no reason why. I became very scared and when I reported to him, I was shaking. He asked me what was wrong. I told him why am I here and he stated you are here for those sergeant test. They asked me 25 questions and I got them all correct. At the end of our meeting I was told that I was a sergeant. At 20 years old I was in control of 18 MP patrolmen.

My present condition is that I always have pain. When it exceeds 8 out of 10, I will take a meds to reduce the pain. If I do not use the meds the pain will continue up until I cannot stand the pain. The pain is in my spine, neck, solders, knees, arms, hands, and feet. Some days my neck hurts and I cannot hold up my head. There is more but this information if enough. I was injured about 50 years ago. I have had a total of 25 surgeries.

After the accident I came to, but I could not see. My sight came back slowly, and I could see color and then blurry things. I then looked up and it looked like the Jeep was falling on me. I tried to climb into a culvert. When I came back and saw the accident site the culvert was only six inches in diameter. Months went by and I got better but I always had extreme pain until I got out of the Army. I could never run or even walk fast. When I got out of the Army, I could walk 50 feet with much pain and then I had to sit down.

I finally could walk and pull patrol. During the time I could not walk I worked on cold cases and settled 6 the first few weeks. The CID wanted me so they could get recognition, but I said no because I had to sign for another year. Because of the pain and no pain pills I needed out of the army. I did make detective because of the cold cases.

I did get better and went to college. In college I got a degree in civil engineering. Working I still had a lot of pain. Then one day brushing my teeth I collapsed on the floor and could not move my legs. The pain was gone for a while. I was taken to the hospital where I was for some time to figure out what to do with my spine. This accident has been many years ago and you must now go to the records and see when all my surgeries took place.

Too much serious talk I must tell you more stories you will not believe. After six months in Germany my brother called from Darmstadt and invited me up. I was in the Bavarian mountains of Southern German. It took me two hours and I was at his company. We had a lot of fun, went to supper, and then sat down and talked. I said how are you doing? He told me that two weeks ago his company was ordered to go for field training in the snow. I ask him how bad the trip was. He said are you touched? it was cold outside, and I am allergic to snow. Well then how did you get out of the trip? When all he said was, I control all the wiring in the building. So, the night before we left, I cut the speaker wires and some electrical wires because I knew they would ask me to stay behind and fix the problems. I told them I had no idea what was wrong and how to fix it. So, when they were out for one week, I slept in my bed. Finally, I told them I could come, they told me to forget it because there is no time left. This was only the beginning of my brother saga.

The next day was Saturday and I said let us go downtown because I have not seen it. We get down the steps and headed for the street where a captain came along, and my brother walked straight towards him. I stepped off the sidewalk, but my brother walks at him. The captain stepped off the sidewalk to miss my brother. I said what are you doing? He smiled and said I am walking down my sidewalk. The captain can use my sidewalk when I am not there. I told him you are going to go to jail. He just smiled and said what will they do send me to Vietnam. And so we went downtown and at some fun. When I got back to his room, his roommate was there. I started by asking him how he liked my brother. I could not believe what he said.

My brother's previous roommate would not take a bath. He told everybody at the office he cannot sleep because of the rotten smell of his roommate. On the third night my brother tried to throw the guy out the fourth story window. He would not do that, but the roommate did not know it. When he headed the guy part way out the window, he had pulled him back and threw him out of the room. He then took the wall lockers containing the stinking belongings and threw he roommate's things where the lockers out the fourth story building window. So you see my brother has a new roommate and I hope we do not fight because it is a long way to the ground from fourth floor. And then the roommate started laughing and that made us to start laughing until our sides hurt.

I said Well is that all you have done. The roommate looked at me and said that is just the beginning and his laughter started and continued until my face hurt. He said I have never met anyone who got kicked off KP to never to return. For those who do not know K P is kitchen patrol. I asked him how do you get kicked off KP duty. Well Jim got kicked out the first time when he mopped the floors. When they told him to do this, he asked where the mop with a bucket and the soap. They said you private it is in the closet. So, my brother gets the water in the bucket and then looked for the soap. This was a big closet and he saw Crisco vegetable oil in a bottle. He finds the soap bottle and he empty out soap out. He then fills the soap bottle full of Crisco vegetable oil. With all that he goes out to the dining area to mop.

But before he does, he asks the sergeant in charge how much so would be named a for his bucket. The sergeant said to put in a cup full, so my brother did. The sergeant had to go to a meeting for 2 hours. It took 20 minutes to map the floor and the rest of his time he drank coffee. Upon the sergeant return the floor was slicker than ice. The third step into the room the sergeant's feet were vertically above him when he fell, he knocked the wind out of his lungs. He lay there for a few minutes moaning. Two guys came over to help him and they both flew across the floor. My brother was removed from duty and I here that made him incredibly sad. At this point we are all laughing, and our sides and faces were going to break. At that point I had to leave the room the pain was too much.

I stayed away for almost an hour and when I returned, they were still laughing and having a good time. My brother's roommate looked at me and said I told you it was just the beginning. For breakfast Jim was to stack the dishes in the plate warmer. Nobody said how high so Jim started to place dishes until he could not jump any higher. The plates were 9 feet high. He started pushing them into the dining area. This time the sergeants said stop so my brother stopped dead in his tracks. Then, 30 plates went flying and broke everywhere. My brother's response was I am so sorry. This time my brother did not return and that meant forever. The sergeant yelled at him until he was out of sight. We all looked at each other and I stuck my head in a pillow and just yelled with laughter. I truly could not take any more, so I went outside. I did not want to go back in. After a few minutes they came outside and said no more tonight. So we went to bed.

The next night started OK but then the stories started again. I told them I am sore and cannot do this again they looked at each other and started to laugh. I turned away because it was starting again. This time my brother's roommate named Bill said you will not believe this. While working on my Brothers Electronics' the new lieutenant told my brother to clean his equipment. My brother looked at him and said you know it is not clean, you do not know what it is. My brother told him it was his own stereo and Electronic Equipment, so the lieutenant said starring and walked away. In fact, you the equipment was for cryptology and top secret. The electronics were in a box because no one could see them unless you had a top-secret clearance. When my brother had the equipment, he had to carry a loaded 45 handgun and would shoot you if you tried to touch it. A few days later the lieutenant walked into the room looked around and walked over to the boxes labeled top secret. My brother turned around to see the lieutenant reaching for the box. My brother pulled his 45-caliber handgun and said stop or I will shoot. My brother told him you are not on my list of people with proper clearance. My brother said I do not know what you want but am required to kill anyone trying to get in classified container. Now get out of the room.

The door has a sign proper clearance required do not enter. Looking down the barrel the lieutenant almost threw up. The lieutenant never spoke or looked at my brother again. Think about it, you think this guy is sane and he walks around with a locked and cocked 45 ACP. After this incident near my brother's captain was afraid. The captain had heard some of what my brother did but there is no proof of anything. Currently we had been in the army for two years. I told my brother they were going to get rid of him. About one month later orders came down for my brother to leave German go home for a month and then report to Fort Lewis for placement in a unit going to Vietnam. I took a few days off and spend with my brother and then take him to the international military Airport.

After I got to his dorm his roommate was there. After that statement we all start laughing again. About 6:00 we headed to my car to go downtown and give my brother his last German meal. Again, the captain was coming up the sidewalk and my brother stated get out of the way and he headed away from us. He truly was afraid of my brother and if I did not know my brother, I would truly be fearful of him.

My brother only had 10 months of service left but they wanted him gone. I would bet anyone that made my brother mad even the officer's lost sleep over him. They had no proof of anything, but they fear him. How would you Eike to have no guns or ammo and be fearful of a person walking around with a loaded gun.

We drove to the Airport at about 3:00 pm. As we drove down the road, I told him to keep Low. He said I am not going to Vietnam. We parked the car and with his duffel bag headed for the terminal. Almost to the building there was a dumpster and my brother said wait here. He simply took his whole file retrieved his plane ticket and threw the file into the Dumpster. As he turned around, I said what are you doing? He simply looked at me and said it will take the army 1 to 2 months to put that file back together. I said how do you know that? He said I did my research and called the paymaster, the medics, and document section and asked them what happens if file is lost. They said we cannot mail military documents because they might be taken by someone, and they would know you have a top-secret rating so they might take you and find out what you know. If we send your document, we put them on military plane until your file gets through to your new unit. I walked him to the plane and told him I am serious keep your head down use what we learned at home on how we learned to evade him at home. Again, he said I am not going to Vietnam. At that time, he boarded the airplane his last words. I will not be going and do not worry. He never did go.

After the jeep accident I could only walk slow and shuffled my feet 10 inches at a time. The pain was getting worse, but I would do anything to have my honorable discharge. Driving back to my unit I had to stop and lay in the grass on the interstate. After about an hour I got into my car and continued. My car was a 10-year-old Volkswagen. The previous owner had used this car for racing. It had a modified porch engine that was amazingly fast. The only law for speed was that you had to limit your speed for safely. I picked up speed and a big Mercedes went by. I continued to accelerate in third gear and was up to 105 miles per hour. I slipped it into fourth gear and went by the big Mercedes. As I did his mouth dropped open. Now I was over 125 miles per hour. This is an estimate because the speedometer only went up to 80 miles per hour. When I had to turn onto secondary roads, I went 20 miles per hour faster than the speed limit. You see that I always had my MP uniform hanging in the back seat of my car. If they stop me, I can apprehend them.

Came home my world was shaken. We had gotten a new po commander and he was a ball Buster. About a week after he took command, he came into my office without knocking and told me that he was taking our second building. This meant we would lose our main day room and must double up bunks. Right now my bedroom was 15 feet wide and 24 feet long with my stereo recording machines, a television, foot lockers, wall lockers and much more. I sat down to ponder my problem. No way would the post commander get the best me. Our commander of the military police was a two-star general, and I remember he had sent a letter to every military police station that if anything happened simply give him a call. I went back to the military police station and found the memo. I said we cannot be any worse off. You must remember that a general is awfully close to the top of the food chain. The phone rang and I became extremely nervous. In fact when the soldier answered my voice squeaked like a mouse. I cleared my throat and explained the serious problem. The person hung up the phone after telling me that he would get back to me. An hour pasted them two. Finally I picked up the phone and it was a sergeant major who was calling for the general. He told me not to worry that he would send somebody over the next day. That left me to believe that the sergeant major would come the next day.

At 2:00 pm we were alerted to accept a helicopter, so we started to set up our defense system. I heard what was going on, so I took our 1965

Chevrolet with a 396 cubic inch motor to the helicopter pad to escort someone to the police station. As the helicopter was landing, I saw that there were two stars. I absolutely could not believe my eyesight. The general climbed out the helicopter and I immediately went to attention and saluted the general. He said you are one of my guys and you did not have to salute me but shake my hand because I hear you have a top-notch office. I opened the car door looked down and my name tag had come loose. The general said do not worry about it and told the first sergeant to fix my name tag clamp. I know the general could see my anxiety and was trying to calm me down.

Finally, we arrived at the military police headquarters. And I was immensely proud to be in charge. After we walked in the front door the general said where is your best office? I directed the general to the office return a genuinely nice high-backed chair. After he sat down, he asked for a cup of coffee. I sent one on my patrolmen to get everyone coffee. The general looked at everybody and said you must relax you are mine and I respect you. For the next hour we explained what was going on and how the new commander hated the military police. After we had said that the general busted out in laughter. The room was silent for almost a minute and the general said go get the police hating person.

We were told by the general to get the post commander but not to say who was at the police station. So, I went over to the post commander's (PC) office and requested time to talk to our military police supervisor. The general had his back to the door so no one could see who he was. The PC pushed his way into the office and said what do you want and have you emptied my second building. The general did not turn around but let the PC spew his mouth. In a split second the general turn and said lock your heels you moron. The PC started to talk, and the general said quite just be silence your mouth. The general looked at me and said send for more coffee and please have a chair. I went over and sat down, and the PC started to move towards a chair and the general snapped lock your heels. We talked for more than 2 minutes and finally the general looked at the PC and said at ease. Which means to stand but to become a little more relaxed. Finally the general told the PC to sit down. The general looked at me and asked can you do without the second building. I said not because the field military police came through the area five or six times a year and usually had more patrolmen than we did. Slowly the general looked at the PC and ask him did you know this? The PC looked down and said no. The general asked him did you talk to Mike about this? Again, the PC looked down and said no. The general looked at him and said if you ever tried to hurt Mike and the patrolmen you will be a private. Now get out of my office and over the next few days you will contact Mike to solve any of your problems. I also order Mike can contact me immediately if you cause any more problems. The PC left the office and the general said I want to see your day room.

Even in our headquarters I have seen pictures of the walls with paintings of the military police in action. We drove down to our building and told the general I presented your beautiful day room. He looked in awe and stated I cannot bring you this room. He requested that we take a few rolls of film and send them to him. We had the photographs developed and picked the best photographs and had a 16" x 24" photo framed.

On another trip to see my Brother Jim I arrived about 5:00 and ask him if you want to go out and get a good German meal. I realized that Jim and his roommate they had been drinking. His roommate looked me and said I will not ruin a million-dollar high on a two-bit sandwich. Oh, my we started laughing. I ask the roommate what they had been up too. I just remembered the roommate named was Karl. Karl looked at me and said absolutely nothing. But did you hear of the rumors going around. I said what do you mean? Well, they said this old Nazis barracks has ghosts and they have been very naughty. They have not hurt anybody, but strange things are happening. I asked what are you talking about? Well things have been missing. I am said what things? Well, when the captain was ready to go home, and his keys went missing. Before long he had 100 men looking for them and someone found them in a mop bucket. Then when that captain got in his car the car would not start so Jim opens the hood and saw that the wires were loose, and he fixed the car so that the Capitan could go home. But the next day the car would not start, and the captain ask Jim was to come to his house and repair the car. Jim is so good that when they took him over, he immediately knew how to fix it. You know the ghosts are getting worse all the time. Someone started rumors about that ghost.

A few days later the captain had been reading a book on military maneuvers during war. When he returned for the book, it was gone.

Pretty soon everybody is looking for the book and where did they find in the attic and hanging from a rope. Again the rumors started. No one was ever caught doing any of this, so it had to be the ghosts. Almost every day things continued to disappear. My brother asks the captain if the ghosts were really in the building. The captain said absolutely no way but when he turned around his gloves were gone.

I am her to say that Jim did not do all these things because he would have been caught. Even back in advanced training the head officer who liked to drive around and throw tear gas grenades found his jeep with four flat tires. It was funny but the officer could not fix the tires because they had been cut by a two-inch-wide blade. After the officer got the tires changed the car would not run because someone put water in the gas tank. Jim always felt bad that the jeep would always break down.

My whole life if someone were playing music I would get upset. I would have to leave the area. I would have lies so why I could not listen to music. No matter what I did I could not listen. Even for as long as I remember I could not listen to music. I went as far as buying a recorder to play music, any music. Then I realized why I could not listen. If I listened, I could not hear anybody coming up on me. Even at six years old I would get upset with music or even a radio playing. Now that I realized this, I tried to remember what happened to make me afraid of sound.

One day I was sitting with a slight headache and had my eyes closed. Someone turned on a radio and that startled me. The idea that after 60 years what people did to me caused this reaction. When this happened, I would close my eyes and try to think of why I reacted so badly. I never have told anybody about this, not even my wife. Again, a radio triggered my response. I close my eyes and I could see a club swinging in my head. I opened my eyes and said what was that?

At our military base I was pretty much in charge of the streets, the clubs, and many other locations. I had it set up so that the patrolmen could go to the movies free, get a free drink at in the club, get a stake or meal for free either downtown or on our base. Then a new captain took over the movie theater, clubs, and other entertainment sites. He came to the MP station and told me everything has stopped. My desk sergeant looked at me and said Well that is the end of a good thing. I told him you give up too easily. Two weeks later I caught a drunk driver. I took the officer to the medics who extracted blood for testing. The officer begged me to give him a chance. I simply took him from the hospital and threw him in jail. I always give people a chance but take free movie passes away by the captain. Every officer on base knew that I was fair but do not go after my patrolmen or me. That week that captain was removed and within a month we had a new captain in charge of entertainment on the base. The previous captain destroyed his career just to be mean.

The new captain came to my office with movie passes and told me to stop by in the club for a free drink and a stake. I wish him a great day as he left. It was not even a week when I saw a car run over a stop sign at the px. I put on my lights and went over to Steve what was going on. Apparently, the new captain had to many drinks. I went over and bent the sign back into place. I ask him how far it to his house was. He said it is the five blocks. I said you are going to get a drunk driving ticket for five blocks. He just looked down on the ground. By then I realized he was not that intoxicated but simply did not see the sign. I ask him to promise to walk home the next time. I looked at the captain and said a buddy will see you tomorrow and I went back to my patrol car. The next day I came into police station to find a dozen donuts filled with vanilla pudding. OK I did share.

I really had a problem with our new lieutenant. By this time, I was the head sergeant. We went to the party in downtown Crailsheim. We started with a glass slipper that held more than one liter of champagne. If you put it to your mouth the wrong way which was the toe up the vacuum in the toe area would hold for a while and then you got ½ liter in your face. As the night went on, I told everyone to get supper, and no one could drive. My rule has been one beer or one drink and no driving or no firearms for 8 hours. The lieutenant thought that there was something between his wife and me. I said NEVER with a married person.

About two days later the lieutenant called me to his office and asked me if anything happened. I asked him what he was talking about. He said you know what happened in the alley. I told him I went out for fresh air and your wife came out to get some fresh air and when she saw me, she just started talking. We are only there for about 10 seconds, and nothing was improper. He looked at me with rage in his eyes. Apparently, this happens before. Maybe two weeks later while on patrol I saw this beautiful woman and when she turned around it was the lieutenant wife. I drove over to say how are you? I did not get out of the car to talk. Finally, I felt it dangerous to even talk and drove away.

Now I had been in the army two years and my patrol partner wanted to go on vacation. So, I put in for two weeks of vacation to go to Italy and swing way south to Rome and back on the east side of Italy, threw the mountains of Switzerland and back home to Germany. A few days later I learned that Sara the lieutenant wife had put in for vacation to northern Italy. The lieutenant was furious and called me to his office. He has told me to explain where I was going on vacation. I said that my patrol partner and I were going to go to Rome Italy. He glared at me and told me to get out of his office.

We started south and made Switzerland the first night. The Swiss people were cold and self-centered. Their foods at the clubs were awful, so we went back to our car and ate sea ration from World War two and they were better. Driving down the interstate I looked over and there was the leaning tower of Pisa. I told Tom to turn off because I wanted to see the tower and the buildings in the area. He would not stop so I grabbed the wheel and turned the car because I weighed more than 50 pound and was three times stronger.

While at the leaning tower read the sign stating enter at your own peril, the structure is not safe. Well, the first thing we did was climb the tower. The tower was white marble and massive. But as we looked around the church was more impressive. The cathedral was 150 feet in diameter. The walls were maybe 60 feet tall with a massive dome. Tom and I spent the next few hours at the site. They had little models for sale but what would I do with it but break it.

Finally, we got in the car and continued south to Rome Italy. We arrived in the city to find young men on scooters trying to give brochures on hotels. We tried to find our hotel which was the YMCA. We never found it, and no one knew anything because their alphabet does not have the letter Y. So, we followed a guy on his little scooter to his hotel. The hotel was genuinely nice, so we got a room that was at least a four-star hotel. Tom said how I want to go to the Pope's pad and see how he lives.

We arrived at the famous plaza and there was the Pope hanging out the window and talking to the people. Tom and I were hungry so on our way to the pope's pad we had bought a gallon of wine and a 5-pound roasted chicken. We got into the plaza went over to the center water fountain and climbed 10 feet up the statue. We moved around until we had a good sitting area. About then the pope was at the window and started to speak. There were more than 50,000 people in the plaza so what does Tom do he starts to interpret the pope and know he does not know Latin. About then I opened the broasted chicken and started eating. Tom opened the wine, and we started our feast. The pope kept talking and Tom kept on interpreting. I looked over and there was Tom throwing his bones into the water fountain. I said what are you doing, and he is said making a wish.

That night we were downtown and could not find the bathroom, so I went down an alley and did my job. Two girls walked by and looked over and said the Italians are disgraceful. I looked at them and said in Italian word and they gave me the finger. In Germany and other countries gas cost $4.00 a gallon but we have gas stamps which costs us 19¢ a gallon. After the war European countries had two furnished to the American army gasoline set at a price of gas in the United States. I had the car, so Tom bought the gas stamps. He ordered four times what we would need in Italy. On our way out of Italy, we pulled into law last gas station fill my car and Tom went inside. He came out and got into the car. And then looked at me and handed me $150 and said I made almost $300 on gas, and I think we should split it. We had spent two weeks on vacation and had done it for no money.

My dream was to go to college get a degree and have a good life. To do this I saved 25% of my pay by buying savings bonds and sending them home. I knew that someday I wanted to buy a car and, in those days, more than $1000 would make a good beginning. Little did I know as soon as my bond got to Sioux Falls from me was spending them. When I got home and found out someone had stolen all my money, what can I do send a family member to jail. I am always planned and was ready to accomplish my goals, but this was a kick in the stomach. I have never gotten any or taken any money from anybody. I supported my family in high school by driving a semi hundreds of thousands of miles. I had given money to every family member when they were in trouble, except my brother Bill. My brother Bill and I were the workers and givers in the family. When I look back my parents never raised me. Here was my brother Bill and my Sisters Mary Ann and Victoria. When people have many children, they never raised the younger children and as they get older the children become the parents and caregivers. I always hear in big families how can you take care of so many children. When in fact, parents did not raise most of the children, the older children raised the younger children.

The idea that my brother Jim was headed to Vietnam weighed heavily on my heart every day. I believe that if a war is just then I will fight it. But this war was designed for big business and political gain. Think about this, political leaders vote for the worst offense which is to support abortion. As I understand it the black population of the United States is not increasing. Many years ago, abortion clinics were set up in Black Communities so that the babies could be killed just like the Jews. The people who set this up are communists. Think about it, who in their right mind would kill a baby right up until they are born. When some people blow up or killed an abortion doctor, is that bad? May the abortion doctor live in shame forever. To the nurses who assist in the killing fields are no different.

Over my lifetime my wife Sheila was an absolute angle. We were together for 45 years and one day I came home, and she was still in bed. At first, I would just take a nap. It was in the afternoon I thought I should check on her, but it was too late. When she was just 21, she went to the doctor and all her pain was from endometriosis. By that time, she had a hysterectomy, we learn that for every year you have the disease the chances of a heart attack go up 5% per year. She had lived with disease for 22 years. She died at the early age of 62. My daughter, Nicole, wanted an autopsy. The autopsy showed that the bottom of her heart was hard and if you were in a surgery room that doctors could not do anything. I still blame myself as I am there to protect but I failed.

To know Sheila just made me smile. She would always give everything she could. An example is there is a head start program in our schools in Sioux Falls South Dakota. Sheila's best friend and she had many of them was a schoolteacher and Sheila would help her in her classrooms. It seems that all schools will blow money on managers that are not needed but will not spent money on the students. They buy computers when the student should learn basic math sciences and English. Anyway, Sheila goes to class the first time and the children cannot go outside because they have no warm close. Sheila goes to the local Pennies and askes the manager to help her buy 27 hats, gloves, winter jackets, snow pants, socks, and snow boots. At that time there was a sale for 30% off. The manager thought for a moment then told her she could buy all the outfits for half of that. That meant instead of $200 she could have every child with everything for $60.00. My wife Sheila yelled for happiness and filled her car. Every year she continued to buy these outfits. She set it up with the manager that if she gave a student a note they could come into the store and get the same outfits. After two years we look at the receipts and where we are spending more than $7,000 a year. In 1980 that was a lot of money, but we were going to help someone anyway. It has been five years since my heart attack. The last five years have been <u>hard and painful</u>. I went to the doctors to find out why my stomach was so painful. I have had pain troubles in my stomach for almost 10 years. All the doctors ever did was give different medicine to calm my stomach, but the pain was always there. One time I went to the doctors they were too busy to see me so that doctor's assistant looked me over. She said I am going to setup an MRI to see why you were having so much pain. I went to the hospital and had an MRI. Immediately I was scheduled for surgery on my gallbladder. What had happened was my gallbladder had died and was being consumed by my body. What should have been a 1-hour surgery was a 3-hour surgery to cut away what was left of my gallbladder. The gallbladder was being consumed and was leaking into my stomach which caused all the pain. After two days I was doing well and was sent home. I arrived home andafter a couple minutes my sons said he was going to go home. I then looked at my son and I passed out. I came to an extreme pain and my son rushed me back to the hospital. The bile was filling my stomach area which caused extreme pain. I was rushed back into surgery and repairs were made by stopping the bile from leaking. When I woke up after surgery, I had tubes in my stomach to flush the bile out. Because of the extreme pain I was sedated and for the next four days remember little. My son in law came into the see me and was shocked because I was near death. Everybody that came to see me ask the doctors if I would make it. The doctors said we do not know.

Finally, after about one week I opened my eyes looked at my kids and gave a weak smile. Finally, they thought I would make it. For the next four weeks I had to go to the hospital to get antibiotics at 6:00 AM, 2:00 PM and again at 10:00 PM. After doing this for two days I told my kids that I would do it myself and they had done a lot. I was too tired to drive my cell bird may be in stubborn tried it myself. The second night I backed into a car and the fourth night I went out to say hi to my brother and backed into a tree. From then on, my son or daughter would take me to the hospital.

After we were married,we have found out that we cannot have our own biological children. One night Sheila came to me sobbing and broken. She asked me for a divorce! I ask her what did I do that was wrong? She said I feel worthless because I cannot give you a child. I told her that I could not give her the divorce because I would be alone because nobody would want me. I laughed a little because the room was dark. We talked and I told her there must be a reason that God allowed this. The next week I called the state and other social services to see if we could adopt a child. I believe we are all children of God and have an awfully specific goal for each person. It is up to us to find our reason for living. She loved children, especially infants. We signed up to be foster parents. Shelia had been babysitting since she was 10 years old. There were some young parents who were not ready to have a child, or my great granddaughter was born.She was beautiful. Her parents were good people and just learning life.

We started to have our great granddaughter Brielle many nights while the parents like to party, see their friends, and have a good time and of course they worked a lot. Sheila even set up the baby's room with everything you could imagine. When her parents would come, Sheila would say she is sleeping and just let her sleep and we will see you tomorrow. And so, I watched this beautiful child grow to a beautiful woman. Sheila had an old convertible and decided that Brielle should have the car for her graduation. We cleaned the old car up which only had 50,000 miles and gave it to add her graduation party. She liked to drive up to the party with the top down the car all waxed up and gave her the keys and the title. Brielle lived with me this last year. With all my heart I was no longer alone. Brielle helped me through bad times, and I will always be thankful. That time has passed but I think back how much she had helped.

I arrived at the police station about 730 PM and prepared to go on patrol. One of those small patrolmen came over to me and said I can't go on patrol with you. He said if we get in a Fight, I cannot help you and you might get hurt. I thought about it and said what you would like to be a desk sergeant? He said it would be a lot safer for everybody. That night even though he was in new, he became a desk sergeant. Two weeks later I was driving by one of the club's and when the door opened there were six guys b beating this small patrolman. I was furious and jumped out of a car to stop the fight. I ran after one of the bigger soldiers and ran but could not catch him. So, I told him to stop, or I would shoot him. The man stopped I told him to get on his knees and when he turned around and I was holding my club but no gun. I took him to the police station and put him in jail.

An hour later I called the hospital, and a little patrolman was still unconscious. I went to the man in jail and told room he would be going to prison them for attempted murder and that he would probably get more than 20 years. My patrolmen or desk sergeant recovered but the man who beat him went to prison. While in jail the man would not tell who he was with. I told the man in jail that the little MP had a friend, and he was going to come down and hopefully not kill him. We sent the biggest MP we had. The patrolmen were 6 foot six and had played professional football. I pretended to try to scare the person and in the back room made all kinds of noises from being beaten by the big patrolmen. We have a lot of laughs but then this here that man took his knife with the keys and home from the cell door. At that time I said we are all leaving, and the big cop was charge. The cop opened the cell door while hitting the knife against the steel bars. The big cop told the prisoner that if you want to kill my partner then I will kill you.

The big cop smashed his nose and put the knife to his throat and started to cut. At that time, the man told him the name of all five of their soldiers who had beaten the small patrolmen. That night we arrested three of the five men and did not take into a jail but transported them to Mannheim military prison. They were all given two years of hard labor. What is hard labor? That is busting rocks for 12 hours a day every day to include Sunday. If not, enough rocks are not broken there will be no supper. It is absolutely a nightmare. Also, there is a never a repeat offender.

I received information on my radio that four men had robbed a young couple and stabbed the young man. The young man was in the hospital and should make it OK. I told the desk sergeant who put out an all-points bulletin and to put roadblocks at 30 miles. I told everyone that we would get these criminals. As people were stopped anyone with four people in the car were taken to the police station. The young girl was brought in and 6 hours later we had them. They were gang out terrorizing the countryside.

Since the four men were German and had stabbed an American soldier, they were taken to the prison and given no rights. When convicted they would be given five years hard labor with no parole.

I was on patrol at 2:00 AM and was very tired. I simply pull the patrol car off the road and fell asleep. I had a dream when I was in a boat at the age of 12. I woke up and started to recall the incident. I have been driving the boat got tired of being in the boat, so I went to the beach area and dove into the water. I did not know but there was a sandbar, and I dove in to only 2 feet of water. Instantly I was in the sky about 200 feet, and I wascalm. I could see my body lying at the bottom of the lake not moving and looked dead. This did not matter because I was calm and felt I was in total control very much liked where I was and wanted to leave my body behind. I had no idea, nor had I ever heard of being an out of body experience.

I could see everything perfectly and I knew I was not looking out of a normal eye. Then my sister Victoria started walking towards my body. I did not want her to get at the body but to just turn and walk away. Victoria had seen me dive but not come up. My sister said I was in the water for more than 2 minutes. Time had passed, and I could see my sister reaching down into the water and finally she started to pull on my hair. I did not feel any of this, but I could see her doing that. Victoria then hit me, and I snapped back into my body and was trying to breathe. The whole time that I was under the water did not go into my lungs. Two other people helped bring me to move the shore and onto a blanket.

After 20 minutes I can finally talk and started to tell my sister Victoria about my trip into the sky. I told her of things that were impossible to know. Across the highway was the old barn and I told my sister that there was an old tractor that had been broken and being stored in the barn. I told her other things that were impossible to know unless I was in the very sky above us. For example, she said no one could find my brother-in-law and I told her he is on the other side of the restaurant eating hot dogs. Later he came back and said the exact words. A few hours later I called my sister that I was going to ask to look inside the barn. When I was in this sky, I could see a john Deere tractor with front broken off.

At the house I ask the older lady if I could see in the barn. She said why would you like to see. I told her about being in the sky and seeing the broken tractor with the front laying off to the west side. The lady said that was true and her husband had been hit by a drunk driver when he was on the tractor on the highway. I went into the barn and the tractor with the same color model and a broken front end and lay just west of the tractor frame. We just stood there and look at each other. Later I would learn about out of body experiences. The details of that experience were seared into my brain.

Many of the patrolmen were sitting in our dormitory talking about old times. Someone brought up high school and singing in a group. I told them my freshman year we had to complete some extra classes for pleasure. I had a priest who was the choirmaster. I asked him what that meant and could I join. I ended up loving choir because it came easy, and no sound were beautiful. A week later I would go out for football and ended up on the varsity team. At 3:00 every day I would go to the choir room and sing with everybody. I finally found something in my life that I genuinely wanted to do. The first football game came, and I was on the team. I am really did not like football because you would fight hard and never touch the ball. I kept playing but did not really like it. Then one day I got on my uniform and headed out for practice. The coach had said why are you always late? I told him how much I loved choir, but I would be late 10 or 15 minutes every day. The truth I liked to go to choir so that did not care if I would be late. I ask coach I would be late for football, and he saidbe on time or be on time or the highway.

I thought for a minute and walked off the field and quit football. Later the coach would ask me to come back and I could be late for a few minutes. I told the coach the game was stupid because I never touched the ball. The coach never asks me again.

When I went into the army one of the questions was about my religious faith. I was asking if I were catholic. I responded no I had quit being a catholic in fourth grade. The army recruiter asked me how that came to be. I was in fourth grade and my best friend was Arthur Cummings and he had of serious heart disease. I would help him with his homework but as time went on, he was only coming to school one or two days a week. Then one day the teacher told me he was in the hospital, so I asked my parents, and they took me to see him. By this time, he was unconscious and not responsive. Two days later he passed away.

At catechism I ask the nun and a priest about going to the funeral. He told me that he was not totally for it and that I should not go to the funeral. I gasp with horror. I asked her why not go because he was my best friend. She said if you must go, do not listen to the preacher, and just set their doing nothing, no standing nor listening. I said to myself my if this is my faith then I don't want it. I would not listen to any priest or nun. That was the end of my catholic faith. I would go through grade school and high school with only one other friend. My junior year the drunk driver killed my other friend. Having a friend was too painful and I kept my distance from everybody after that.

Since I was ahead of hard patrol group, I ask everybody to work for 10 days in a row and then we could take off 4 days in a row. This worked out great until we were told to set up communications as though we were at war. Our unit did not have enough people to do this because some of the patrolmen were in Switzerland and other countries having fun. I realized if I could not set it up there would be my court martial. I called some German friends, explained that the situation and that all agreed to help. Well I thought if we were at war my friends would help me. Different guys read the instructions and drove off in military vehicles and military uniforms. I had really could be in trouble but thankfully the German men and women could also speak English maybe better than me.

We pulled it off, passed our mission and looked very professional and was given one of the high marks for our response. After it was over, I threw a party for everyone involved where everyone laughed.

Every year every unit would have an inspection by the inspector general. These were always given with no warning except we were a police unit which was on duty 24/7. About eight months before it got to my unit, they had an inspection had failed the inspection and had to have a new inspection every three months until they performed at a higher level. I had other patrolmen who were smaller and had never been in a fight. He begged me to put him somewhere because he could not fight anybody. After I heard this, I put him in charge of all records and documents for our unit as well as preparing for the IG inspection. I even gave him a jeep that he would use by placing it in the motor pool and never taken out of the building. He would take that jeep jacket it up and spin miles on the engine.

He would go to the arms room and clean every pistol and rifle and any other equipment for the inspection. A few months went by, and we were told the inspection was coming. I prayed that our efforts would pay off. We went through the inspection by calling and falls our actions, so everyone was gone except this person. If a person is not present none of his belongings or area can be inspected. Two weeks later we got the evaluation and for the first time in the history of our battalion we were rated Exceptional. By getting to this level everyone in the army in Europe became aware and all the officers in our unit looked Exceptional. Later and just before leaving Germany I was asking by my commander how I pulled it off. Finally, I told him about having one person for the inspection and everyone else to stay away and we had agood laugh.

Six months ago, I was sitting at home and my son came over to see me. I looked at him and said I am going blind. He said what? And I said my vision is going away and know I cannot see anything. It looks like a kaleidoscope of bright colors everywhere. My son called my doctor and he said go to an eye doctor and he will be waiting for you. We went to the surgeon and took a few simple tests and said go to the emergency room is not your eyes. We got to the emergency room and the doctors talk to me for about 1 minute and I was off to an MRI. An hour after that I was in the surgical ward where I was put to sleep. About one day later I started to wake up and I had a very blurry vision. I had a stroke. Apparently, the blood flow to my brain had been restricted and caused my vision to stop working. I have been recuperating for six months and my vision at more than 5 feet has returned but closer things are blurry, and I cannot read. According to the doctors my sight will slowly return.

I have been pulling patrol for a few hours and pulled by the class six door (Alcohol store). That class six door is the base door where you can get alcohol. Everyone in the army gets a book and when you buy alcohol you have to have a stamp that you take care of the book. So, every time you buy a bottle you must peel the tab off, and the stamps are turned over to show that someone can legally obtain the alcohol.

We were on the scene of an accident and the driver was taken to the hospital. My partner went through the car and found class 6 coupons with 100 booklets that can be used in the class six store. My partner through the books back into a car and had the car towed to the base. At that time, we went back on patrol.

A few weeks went by, and I was on patrol doing school crossing. As I was watching cars, I saw a new Mercedes sports car coming doing 70 mph in a school zone. I believe the car was a 280 S L. They told me that his new German wife's family had bought it for him. I said oh that is nice, but I knew that was no true because the family did not have that kind of money. I confronted him to tell me what was going on. He finally told me that he went back and got all the class six booklets. He went to the class six store and was buying alcohol and taking it home.

Then the bars in town would bring the empty bottles and put the new alcohol into the German bottles. He was buying the bottles for under $1.00 a quart of the alcohol. Whiskey in Germany was awfully expensive so that alcohol cost 46 dollars and he sold his alcohol for $23.00 for the same alcohol. He had been doing this for a few months and that was how he bought the car. I told him he could go ahead and do it, but I would not get involved. He stayed in the area and continued to be an MP for the next 20 years continuing his business. Years later he told me that his German wife wanted to stay around her family. He continued the business all the time he was in the army and made more than one million dollars.

When I was on patrol, we got a call to go to the class six store. The new manager went through his warehouse to inventory and found that more than 600 cases of alcohol were empty. But with no proof of anything I let it go. Whoever got the alcohol made $ 10,000. Within my partner bought a new house for cash. To me my patrol partner was making thousands of dollars every month. The house was better than all the houses in that area. I went to his house and ask him where he got the money. He laughed and told me that I had turned down his new business. I could not believe how much money he was making. But I would never do anything illegal.

I was getting ready to retire and was home on Saturday. Five years ago, I got a bad headache like I had never had before. The headache was so bad I went to my car and headed for the hospital. While I was driving the headache got worse and I could not see out of my left eye. Only one block from the hospital my right eye vision started to go blind. Finally,I went into the emergency room and fell.

The nurses picked me up and put me on a bed. The doctors came and after talking to me the doctor send me to get an MRI. Within an hour I was sent for open heart surgery. The doctor said that 1 out of two hundred people having a heart attack had symptoms of a severe headache. I could not believe the expertise of the doctor knew what I had in less than 2 minutes. When I went two surgeries, they tried to put stents into my heart. But they could not get them in because the artery was so full so had to open my chest. My recovery they went terribly slow but after three months I was back to myself.

My best friend and moved north and I went to see him. His wife was a nurse and we talked about covid epidemic. I told her I could not believe how many people were dying from this disease. She looked at me and said all the numbers are inflated so that hospitals could get a lot more money. I said what are you talking about? She said no matter who dies of Covid, they always put the disease for the person dying. She said a man was 92 years old and dying because of a bad heart. Without testing the doctor looked at him and said he had covid and put that on his death certificate. Based on what she saw more than 60% of the people dying did not die of covid but of natural causes like a typical heart attack. She said when she talked to friends that were nurses from Minneapolis to forgo down to Windom Minnesota those same things were happening and more of an 50% of the death were something different than covid epidemic.

After my stroke I finally could see although everything was very blurry, and I could not see up close I was sort of happy and laying there on and strong medication I fell asleep. It seemed like I started to dream, and it was the dream I had for years I would see something or someone and start running. I would look around but could never see anybody but this time I saw that young girl face, and she was a paid babysitter that my folks had hired when they went for two weeks to weeks to California. She ran after me and when she caught me, she hit me extremely hard on my head. As soon as she hit me on the head I woke up.

I stayed in bed but my memories of long ago were finally coming back. When the girl hit me on the head, she said that I deserved it. I remember when she woke me up it was 3:00 AM. When she hit me, I could see stars, but she grabbed me by the arm and pulled me up extremely hard and now my head and arm was throbbing. I told her I wanted to go to bed. She said: good time but now you need a bath. We went into the house, and she pulled out the tub. She dragged me over to the tub and took my clothes off and she hit me hard in the head and started to beat my butt.

I started to scream but she put her hand over my mouth and pinched me hard on my arm. I stop screaming but she hit me hard on the head. I lay on her lap, and she starts to feel me all over. She seemed to be nicer but then she started to get me up and hit me hard on the head. I fell and hit the stove and I was unconscious. I wanted to go to bed when she said get in the tub. I slowly went towards the tub when she hit me on the side of my head. I woke up the next day in my bed with a bad headache. I tried to get out of bed, but my arm hurts so bad, and my headache hurt, and I was hungry and just fell back into bed. I was only five years old when this happened to me. I just stayed in bed so I would not be hit again. I heard someone coming up the stairs, so I put a blanket over my head pretended to be asleep. Then I heard a voice and she said good morning sleepy head and I knew I was safe because it was my big Sister Mary.

My older brothers and sisters were staying at friend's house for sleepovers. I slowly got up put my clothes on and made my way outside so nobody could see in me. Once outside I started running to a neighbor who was a mile away. I ran a long way and fell in a heap exhausted. Then I heard her voice. I tried to ruin but there was no reason to run someone hit me in the head. Then I realized I would be alone with her many more days. It made me terrified, but I would not cry because I was a big boy.

On the way back she would knock me down until I could not get up. Finally, she grabbed my arm the one that hurts so bad and started driving me to the house. She said you have been a bad person and I will have to spank you. She said I was dirty and needed a bath. She brought out the tub and filled it with water. Slowly she took off my clothes and started to rub my back and bottom. She reached between my leg and started pulling. That is more than I can take, I must stop. Well, the abuse continued for days.

I remember pulling patrol when we got a call to hear two men who had broken into a store and stolen watches and other jewelry then left the area. Someone had seen them and new who they were. It was on last Saturday night about 11:00 pm. The two men were beside each other preparing to go to bed. My patrol partner was a huge black man who had played college football at Colorado, and he looked really tuff. I was awfully glad that that he was on my side. We approached the two men when from behind me a man hit me on the head extremely hard and I collapsed and was knocked unconscious. I woke up in the ambulance and saw another ambulance putting a soldier in it. I asked my partner who the other man was. He said he was the guy that hit you with a bottle. I said what did you do? When he hit you, I took after him and I hit him with a cross body block on him into the big metal register. I hit him so hard they do not know if he will live. The next day I was still in the hospital and ask how the other soldier was doing. They told me that he finally came to, but he has a broken collarbone five broken ribs and a punctured lung. After I could get out of bed I went over to another soldier and ask why he hit me. He said I was picking on his friend, and one had to stop us. Later he was sent to Mannheim military prison for two years because he had attacked an MP and had sent him to the hospital. What is bad about going prison is that you still are back in the army to complete your contract and you start at the bottom private. With a history of aggravated battery will never get any rank but must put in your time. Most of the soldiers who did this went automatically to Vietnam.

Some of the Germans on the back roads would drive so fast and dangerous we were asked to set up road control at the place where the kids crossed the secondary highway which went to their houses. Before we control the traffic some of the older kids would put up a stop sign when the kids crossed the road, but the Germans would go amazingly fast and not stop for anything. I volunteered to come in early before my night shift to help the kids cross the highway. The kids started across the highway when a speeding car came around the corner and appeared not to slow down or anything.

I yelled at the kids to get back and as the car went by me, I took my club which had 10 ounces of lead in the end and broke the front headlight and dented the fender then continuedto break the windshield. The man was so mad he came back to yell at me. I ask him if he had seen the children crossing the road. The man answered yes and the kids to get out of the road. I lost it and my club hit him alongside of the head. When he woke up, he was laying in the grass with his hands cuffed behind him. He starts yelling at me again, so I went to my patrol car got in the trunk and found shipping tape. I had put it on his mouth and gently kicked him in the head which gave him a black eye.

When the German police came, they looked at the man and said he is an especially important man. I said no he is not he is a prisoner who will be charged with attempted murder of the children. They said we cannot do that! I told them if you cannot I can. Another patrol car pulled up and I told them, because I was in charge, to take the prisoner and lock him up and the charges are attempted murder of a child. Yes, he was a captain in the SS.

They looked at me and said if he is convicted that would be a life sentence or at least 30 years. After I got back to the police station, I checked on my prisoner and he wanted to call a friend. I told him that I would do that, but it might take a week or more. The cooks had to bring three meals a day to a prisoner. I told them that I would take care of this. So when I got his first meal, I took a loaf of bread and a jar of peanut butter to him with a quart of water. He said I need more than this. I told him that I would investigate it the next two week and closed the big door to the prison cells where you could yell all day, and nobody could hear you screaming.

Two days later I went back to his cell and said you can have your phone call to your lawyer. He called his friend, a lawyer, and the German police. I instructed all my patrolmen if anybody comes in to see my prisoner, tell them to wait and call me. When the patrol got me on my radio, I took 2 hours to get back to the station. After I arrived, they were all hopping mad, and I told them to leave the police station, or they would be put in the jail cells. This calmed them down fast. They wanted to get their friend out of jail. I told them what the charges against him were and that was not possible however they could go to my commanding general and plead his case. I called the commanding general and explained what I had done. All he did was laugh and he said tell them that the bail is set at $100,000.

Apparently, this German worked in town at his business and drove this road every day. Finally, I called his friends and lawyer to talk about releasing him from jail. I ask him if he felt he was at fault for driving like amad man. He put his head down and said he would never do it again. I told him that he could never drive any place the children were at which meant instead of 8 miles home instead it would be 24 miles. I instructed anyone on the crosswalk for the children to apprehend the driver if he ever used this road. As far as we know he is still driving 24 miles to get home.

We were on patrol when we got a call on the radio. We were to go to the rendezvous point. After we arrived in the park our good friend was there. He told me we would start to move the warheads into an area which would defend areas North of our sector. We ask if he had any information where we would take the nukes to. He gave us a map which showed the distribution of all the warheads. There would be 7 nuclear warheads to remain in Crailsheim Germany. The map showed that we would take about 7 warheads to each location designated on the map. The areas were north of our safe area and over the last year new storage safes had been built. In addition, new artillery guns had been set up at each of our drop areas. We were given combinations and locations to move the warheads to their locations. After we would place the nuclear war heads in each safe someone designated would control them. After our meeting we headed back to the police station to figure out how we would transport the warheads. We would start with the closest location which was 40 miles north. But we ask ourselves how transport with the old Nazis and Russians everywhere?

I see the General in my office with the map location for our deliveries. The person on the other end said do not say anything but meet me at our rendezvous point at the guest house but had a message to go to the second meeting spot. I went to the park and a new person was there, he said here is a list of each time you move the war heads. Here is a radio that will talk to 2 helicopters set up as gunships. They will stay 5 miles from your vehicle but will be able to see you all the time. If anything should happen, they will kill everything in sight but your truck. We have brought an old milk truck or refrigeration truck to move every war head to the safe area. Use this truck to transport all the weapons one location at a time.

The day before I was to start transporting, I went to the safe building and looked at the truck we were going to you use. It was old but in good shape. The truck was full of gas, and it started as soon as I turn the key. The next morning, I went to the truck, and it was already loaded with the warheads. I never saw any person around it, but I was ready to travel. I was to leave the front gate add exactly 9 AM and precede to our first drop off point. On my map there was a route to follow on the roads. I was maybe 10 miles down the road when I noticed the 2 helicopters flying about 5 miles away and about 5000-foot elevation. I do not know how but they were watching me as we traveled. An hour later I arrived at the designated drop point. When I arrived there was a person who gave me the correct word so I could trust him, and I let him into the truck. He said go to the px and get some food and the truck will be ready for you in 20 minutes. When I returned there was no one there and the truck was empty. I started the truck and headed for home.

All the time that I was delivering these weapons I had worked 24 hours shift but had slept so I could make deliveries. Every delivery went off like clockwork. I was happy the last day that I had to deliver anymore weapons to designated areas. That night when I got on patrol at 8 PM I realized we still had the bigger nuclear weapons in the safe. About a week later I got a call to go to the park for a meeting. I headed to the park and met with the new guy who handed me a map with instructions on how to deliver the larger bombs. With the same instructions I would leave with one bomb at 9 AM in the morning designated on the report. I would travel east to the Czech border where someone would meet me and take the weapon over the border. I had no idea where it was going but based on my knowledge it was going into Russia.

The last time I was in the safe there were more larger bombs, but I had never seen anyone round that building. They must come when no one is there. I continued delivering the bombs to the designated areas. Every time I would go to the truck, I would have the truck loaded and all I did was it drive it to the next rendezvous point.

A few weeks had passed, and then my serious accident happened. When I came to there was a person that I had never seen. He asked me how I was doing. It was coming in and out of consciousness. He said I will be back in a few days. Then the nurse gave me a shot and I went to sleep. More time had passed, and the person returned to talk with me. He said with your problems you will probably get a medical discharge. I told him that I would not get a medical discharge but would stay in the army. He said we have another person that will take your place for now.

We talked a little bit more, and he said I must go. We will watch you and if you did a lot better, we would contact you again. If for any reason you are a lot better just call on the radio at 8:00 AM and tell me there is a meeting. I had one question and ask him if he would tell me where are a big bomb located? He looked at me and said with your Clearance, I can tell you. The second bomb was taken and is now within 4 miles of the

Kremlin. If war starts, everything in Moscow will disappear. I said thank you and hope we do not need to use the bombs.

It seems ridiculous that since we were not in a war zone, we would not get medals for any of our efforts. Two of our guys were shot while working with nuclear weapons near the eastern border. Apparently, a Russian spy was observing our soldier and could not find out what he was doing. Apparently, someone gave the order to take him out, but he was lucky and had a bullet proof vest on. From then on, we would only operate in a building so no one could see anything.

A few days later, my patrolmen came to the hospital to get me. I was in a lot of pain, but if I said that I needed a pain reliever I would go back to the hospital and get a medical discharge. I told my partner that I was in a lot of pain. In the next town he pulled into a parking area and said he would be back. He came back and got in the car and handed me a bottle of German beer. It tasted good and when I finished it, the pain was a lot lower, and I could stand the pain easier. By that time, we got to our police station I was very tired and in pain. I would not believe that I would be in pain for the rest of my life.

The nightmare continued my whole life since I was four years old. The nightmares profoundly changed my life. No matter what I did I always had my back to the wall or kept looking around to make sure no one could sneak upon me. I would not even listen to music or be around anyone who listened to music. It makes it so I cannot hear anybody coming. When I finally got into high school I would listen to the radio while driving a truck because no one could sneak up on me. While driving a truck you have a lot of time to think. When I thought that I did not listen to music to make sure that I was OK it really made me mad. The idea that I did not have a childhood nor normal high school years to mess around made me even madder.

I had only gone to one dance with a date in high school. I did have a beautiful girl that would come over to the sale barn and spend time with me when I would load out cattle from the sale. She was a lot of fun and we spent a lot of time together. When I told her I was joining the army I told her I would be home within the year and to wait for me. I came home for the month but for some reason I never got to call her. Someone wrote me that she had found her dream guy and had gotten married. I always wished she had waited for me. Another thing that made me laugh with the kids in high school thought I had this glamorous job of driving, drinking, and having fun. I worked day and night never doing anything wrong.

When I was a freshman, a senior came into the library and pushed my books on the floor. I told them to a pick them up and he said make me. I went over got my books and put them back on my desk. While doing this he hit me extremely hard in the back. I reacted by whirling around and hit him in the jaw which made him hit the wall and he fell to the ground. The teacher came in the room and the only he saw was me hitting him in the jaw. He ordered me out of the room and asked me why I did it. I explained to him that the seniors could hit anyone, and they were scared to tell anybody. The teacher was also my coach and knew that I was not a person that would hurt anybody unless the other person started something. He told me to go to an empty classroom because of the other guy was mad. I thought that was the end of the problem.

A few days later after football practice my brother Jim and I were walking to our car. My Brother Jim got in the car and a few guys held the door shut and six more seniors started to beatme. After they had knocked me down, they started kicking sometimes in the face. They had kicked me in the head so badly my left eye was swollen shut and my right eye was open a small amount. They stopped beating me, but I could not get up when suddenly two priests came down to help me. A few minutes later the police arrived and interrogated the other students.

I finally got up part way and went and sat in the car. Finally, I told my brother to take me home. I missed the next two days of school. When I went back to school a police officer came to the school to talk to me. He had a list of all the students who had held my brother in the car and those six who beat me. He took photographs that really looked bad I have eyes swollen cuts on my forehead and black eyes.

When I went from class to class the eight students could not be found. After about a week I saw them walking around. A week later the police came to my house and ask me to go see a judge. The judge said that seven of the students were 18 years old and classified as adults. He asks me to sign a formal complaint which I did. The eight students came to see the judge and to see how they would plead. Of course, everybody pleads not guilty. About a week later one on my teachers in grade school came to my house and she was crying uncontrollably. My mother brought her in and sat her down. It took a few minutes for her to calm down and talk. One of the students who beat me was her son. She said she had seen the photographs of how badly I had been beaten. She said that you were not to blame if I made them go to court and then they would be sent to prison.

I absolutely loved this teacher and did not want to see her cry anymore. After about an hour she got up and left. Another week passed and the patrol car came to the school and requested that I go see a judge. I went into the judge's chambers, and he explained everything that was going on. He said in a week two there with the court and without a doubt the eight students would end up in prison. He said if this happens their careers are over. He said he wanted a cup of coffee for me to set their and decide what I was going to do. He said that if nothing more happened, they still had a record of assaulting a minor. I thought of my teacher, and it could literally crush her because of her son. I told the judge that these eight students were hurting people all the time. They would scare them knock them down or anything they wanted to do. I knew now that they could never do anything to anybody.

I ask the judge could he set a trial date and make them sweat for the next two weeks. And then I would drop the charges for now and if they did not do anything for the rest of the school year it would be over. But if they did anything they would end up in prison. I saw them back in school and they would look at the ground and no one else. I told my brother the two who had kicked me in the face would get a beating. I waited for my chance to get them alone and one of them was late for class and when he came around the corner,I punch him in the face as hard as I could. He hit the ground and I jumped on him and continued to smash his face. When I was done, he could not open his one eye. I thought to myself one down and one to go. I passed my brother in the hallway and he said follow me. We went further down the hallway and there was the second one leaning against a wall and not paying attention. My brother walked up to him and struck him in the head so hard that guy collapsed and did not move. I said I hope you did not kill him. The guy moved a little, so we got out of the area. Later we saw the second guy being helped to a car to go home. From then on, all eight students walked in fear of my brother and me. We knew they could not gang up and get us because that meant prison.

My whole life no matter what I was doing I would start thinking about my childhood and would go into almost a trance. I would not talk to anybody for hours but stayed in a trance. I had been lonely my whole life trucking, working in the fields or feeding the animals. I did not like being alone anymore and one Saturday I went over to my brother's apartment. There was a beautiful blonde talking to my brother. I ask him if this was his girlfriend, and he said no it's the other blond. I started to talk to her, and we really got along. We had gone out for two weeks and I really liked having her in my life. I was short on money this summer of my freshman year in college. I got a call to go to Chicago with a loaded of hogs.

So, I took it and headed for Chicago where one of my MP buddies lived. When I arrived in Chicago, I gave him a call and he ask me where I was. He said do not move I am on my way. He picked me up and said were going to have the best weekend you ever had. I told them I had to be back on the road tomorrow and they all just laughed. He took me into a bar on the south side where he had grown up and introduced me to his brother who owned the bar. He told me that anything I wanted was free. And then his brother said the other guys had a double and they all laughed and started a great night. At midnight, the one brother said let us go fishing and so were jumped in this truck, hooked up the boat and headed for the big lake. I had never seen the skyline at night, and it was magnificent. We motored in the river and looked at the multistory skyscrapers. We never did fish but cruised around looking at the beautiful skyline.

Well, I spent three days with them and finally got back to my truck and headed home. When I got there the owner of the truck was mad, I went over to my car and left the area.While I was away my girlfriend saw a 68 Camaro just like I drove with a girl setting on the council. Immediately she thought I was not driving truck but out on the town with someone else. She drove fast and finally got up beside him and started to yell and realized it was not me. She felt like a fool and would never tell me, but her girlfriend did tell me, and everybody was laughing.

This girl friend would end up being my wife. I had told her how bad my childhood had been. Early on she realized that I would go into a trance and block everything out for hours. Finally, she saw me in this state, she would say where are you, come back. She would continue saying the same thing and I would suddenly snap back. But before this project I would tell you that my childhood was not great but OK. Now that I have started this project, I cannot believe what I am remembering. From being beaten for over a week at four years old to other injuries I had sustained. I am incredibly sad that this world has so much evil, and it is everywhere.

Another day on patrol and were called back to the police station. I receive a telephone call from a German. He does not speak English and I am trying to understand what he is saying. I got that he was a farmer on the south side of town, and something happened in his barn. I gave the phone to other patrolmen and weran out of the building. 5 minutes later we pulled into the farm and the old guy is waving at us to come over. We still do not understand what he is saying that by his action and told my partner to head to the barn and pull your weapon. Slowly we approached the barn and inside we could not believe you what we saw. It was a soldier who was doing something to a caw. I won't discuss this again. I thought to myself there is no way I am going to catch this guy and write a report. We opened the barn door and the guy looked at me. I had seen this person on base. He pulled up his pants and went out the other door and started running fast. I told my partner forget the idea of catching him because I will not write that report. And the man ran down the hill and started going across the frozen river. I yelled at the man to stop and that we would not arrest him. As I saw him cross the river, I could see the ice breaking but he had made it to the other side with only his feet wet. The man could have died from doing this stupid stunt.

We got a call on the radio to see what was going on, so I said it was some German kids pelting rocks at the old farmer. We gave chase after them but slowed down to let them go. I knew the kids from base and could find them on base, but I wanted no part. I would contact their parents.

I have been working on my book or what I call a project for over two years and hoping to be done in another six months. When working on my project I remembered the memories flooding in about my wife Sheila. Sheila loved taking care of seventeen premature infants. A typical baby that we would have would be one day or four weeks old. It was fun and we always gave them a name. The 9th baby we got was a little boy and weighed in at 3 pounds 2 ounces. We gave him the name of Andrew. At his weight it required feeding about ¾ of an ounce every hour.

Sheila took care of him during the day. I would take care of him during the night. I would hold him in the old rocking chair and would set up 5 bottles on the end table. When he started to fuss and move around, I would give a bottle to him and rock. After he finished his bottle, he would fall asleep, and I would fall asleep with him. All night he would wake up and move which woke me up and we continued this all night. Sheila would not take money for any of our services. After about a month we started to get attached to the baby. Then another month went by, and we were more attached to him. By the end of three months, we got a call from the state where they had a family who would adopt Andrew. We talked to each other and said I do not think I can do this again. Three months is too long.

Finally, we got a call to go and get our new baby. Sheila had called me that it was time for our first child. I got excited, left work we went downtown and kicked out a white fur baby sack with a hood. It was gorgeous and expensive. I was so excited I pulled out of the parking lot and a friend of mine ran out into the street waving both hands. He said, "You are going down a one way the wrong way." We both startle laughing and I told him that good news about her new daughter. Everybody says that Nicole was the most beautiful baby.

Nicole would be our first baby and between Sheila and my mother-in-law and I did not get a chance to hold her very much. So, I sat on the sideline and smiled. It was greatbeing a papa. I usually went to work at 4:00 AM so I could get my reports completed when no one was there to bother me. After that I went to see clients and complete engineering projects. I always was home at by 530 pm to be with the family.

All my life I would read books on science. I found a book which tried to define dark matter. The best way to define this work is by example. We send a spaceship into space in the area where the temperature of the earth did not affect samples of what is in outer space. A sample was taken and returned to earth. The sample contained nothing. When in outer space the temperature was 4° Kelvin. Everywhere they went it was 4°. Think about this! There is nothing there, but it has the temperature of 4°everywhere. We will come back to this. Calculations have been made of the milkyway which is where earth is located. They found that a force is required to hold all the planets and suns together. In other words, this force is there but we do not know what it is. The force is everywhere. For many years scientists have tried to define and complete testing even with the collider. Now we have a force which is everywhere but cannot figure out what it is made of. If the temperature out there is 4°, the amount of energy to keep space at a constant temperature is huge or infinite.

In the bible it states that God is in us, around us and everywhere. The force we talked about is in us, around us and everywhere. We cannot see it, test for it but we know that it is there. Please think about this!

Before I go on, I want to make a statement about the governor of South Dakota. Kristi Noam is the governor who is an excellent person who follows the constitution as close as she can. She had nothing to do with the next subject I will explain. She did not have anything to do with the corruption at the state level.

My wife and I received a letter from Governor Janklow where he praised the work and effort that my wife and I had put into new so many premature babies. They were nice to take the time to acknowledge the good work of people like us. When we started the adoption of our son the law stated that the child must be return to the hospital where the child was born. So when he got to over three pounds, we had to drive to Rapid City, South Dakota which was 350 miles. We knew we were going to get a premature baby with many problems, and we know he was in intensive care, so we went to the Sioux Falls hospitals and saw him. Ryan had to be taken by air ambulance from Sioux Falls to Rapid City regional hospital.

We had to get in our car and drove 350 miles in a snowstorm. Since we were well versed on premature infants, we stayed at the hospital for one day. We took Ryan to our car with a breathing monitor and a heart monitor and headed for a Sioux Falls. Usually a 6-hour driving time but because of the snow and snow packed rough roads we would be a on the road for more than 13 hours driving time. The worst part. The interstate was closed.

My wife got mad that the state had spent more than $10,000.00 to fly Ryan from Sioux Falls to Rapid City by an ambulance from Denver Colorado. My wife sat down and composed a letter to Governor Janklow. Dear Mr. Janklow, it went. I am glad (sorry)to see money being wasted because we had to get our son 350 miles west when we observed him in a Sioux Falls hospital. But we could not get him in Sioux Falls but had to drive to Rapid City because that was his origin at birth. The state of South Dakota spent more than $10,000 to complete that journey. We could have drove 4 miles to a hospital in Sioux Falls and picked him up.

In addition, when babies are put up for adoption it can take months for a decision by the mother. We absolutely know how difficult this decision is to make. However, many of the babies are adopted out so that this time for deciding must be minimized both for the mother and for the baby. This decision should not linger for months.

Well within a few months a law was passed where the baby could be placed from any state organization that handles adoption. In addition, that time for the mother's decision was reduced to, I believe, three days. We got a letter from the governor thanking Sheila for her effort to save wasted money and, also to get the babies to their new families as soon as possible. Sheila worried about the three-day limit, so she went to state of South Dakota, Lutheran and Catholic adoption agency and met with many of the young girls to discuss the three-day limit. Out of 24 young girls giving birth only one said she needed more time. Sheila went to this young girl when she was giving birth and the next day wanted to know what her decisionwas? The young girl started crying so Sheila pulled up a chair took her hand, and both were silent for more than an hour. It was lunchtime, so Sheila went out of the hospital and obtained a big juicy burger and fries for the young girl.

Sheila returned the next day because that young girl had no family in the area, and she was alone at 18 years old. All day long Sarah was talking with Sheila. Sheila told her that if the baby is given to a mature mother that would be good. Sara had told Sheila she did not have any work and was living in a rundown apartment with her boyfriend. The boyfriend did not want anything to do with the baby. The boyfriend was only 18 years old and not stable. Sheila went on explaining how she had gotten her daughter and son. Sheila knew it would be hard to watch the baby leave but both would have a better life. The third day came, and Sara decided to adopt the baby out. Sheila stayed with Sara the rest of the day. Sarah had to get ready and go home. Sheila asked her if you want to go home with us. Sarah told Sheila I have no home no parents or my drunken boyfriend. Sheila looked at Sara, but Sara was crying. Sheila told Sara I have a solution do you want to hear it? Sara said why not I have ruined my life. Sheila pulled her tightly into her arms and then both cried for a while.

Sheila had decided that Sara could not go back to where she had been so when the car and drove in it was my wife and Sara. Sarah lived and learned to cook and bake with Sheila. Finally, we got home with Sara who stayed with us for a few months. I went in the house and Sara said do you like my car? Sara had gotten a job and was saving all her money to buy a car. Sheila was tired of driving Sara to work. Sheila went to one of her friends and bought a car. She told Sara she could pay her back in the future. I knew what that meant Sara would get the car.

A few more months have passed, and Sara was promoted at the hospital. We knew that she was making rather good money and we would lose her but not completely because she had become my daughter. Sara had become a new person with a positive outlook and a great future. One night we were sitting around with both babies in bed I ask her a very personal question. What do you think of when you found out you were pregnant? By now Sara was confident and understanding of the whole problem. She looked at me and the tear formed in her eye. My boyfriend wanted an abortion where I did not want to go to that extreme and kill a baby. Did you ever think you might have an abortion? The thought was in my head, but the idea of cutting up a beautiful baby so I would not have a problem was not the solution. I had a decision to make, do I carry it? I know someday a child might look me up and I can tell them that I saved his life from misery. I can tell him that I loved him so much that I cannot keep him.

I have been told law seek justice, where is it. An attorney is a member of the judicial system, if he sees anything illegal, he must stop the procedure. An attorney is like a law officer only he does the prosecution and seeks honesty and justice. Now if an attorney is part of the conspiracy, then he should lose his license. The attorney for the license board in this case heard all evidence to my case about my license. I ask the question to the board that follows: I was standing in front of the board at the hearing when I asked "tell me if I did anything wrong in my engineering for this building? No one would answer. I asked one member what I did wrong? He said I think you did the soils wrong. I told him I was never on this site, and I never wrote any report for the soils on this project. I did absolutely nothing on this project in relation to geotechnical engineering.

Back to the attorney where he observed everything even their structural engineer who stated there was no structure deficiencies. My expert, Mr. Downs, talk to their structural engineer and both agreed that my project was designed correctly. Therefore, they should never take my license. The attorney heard everything and understood everything, but would he tell the board that the license should not be taken. But our justice system is broken. If you do not believe it is broken, my attorney put this case to the Supreme Court. There are so many rules that the real content for the Supreme Court is clouded and cannot be understood. The whole system including the board all failed justice.

I had lost my beloved Sheila which made it hard for me. Sheila was always my savior to get me through hard times. Then I thought maybe it is better she is gone and to see me hurt so bad because of crooked people. Someday, I will be in heaven because when I was young, and I was almost killed when diving out of the boat and hitting the bottom. The water was only 2 feet deep, and I was unconscious when my spirit rose about 200 feet in the air, and I could see all around all the time. It was not like an eye with only a focal point but something where you could see everywhere all the time. I did not want my sister to save me. I could see her walking towards me, but I wanted her to stop and let me go. You will never know what I felt. The calmness I felt had no words it was complete and totally calm in my heart. I have lived a long time but have never felt anything like that. In addition, I had no idea that other people have had out of body experiences. I cannot say enough how incredible that journey was.

Well, I need to tell you how everything started. After we were married, I would have nightmares and my wife would shake me until I was awake. Finally, she called for an appointment with a psychiatrist. I went to a psychiatrist and told him about that terrible dreams and flashbacks I would get scared, but I knew they could not be a real. The doctor talk to me for about an hour and told me they might or might not be true but if you want them to stop and I want you to see another doctor and she might help you.

And told my wife what the doctor had told me, and I went off to work. When I got home, I had an appointment with the new doctor. I went to the doctor for about two months and all that time she wanted me to take notes about my dreams and the flashbacks that I would have time. So, I never started to write a book, but I just kept notes. Finally, she told me she wanted to put me under hypnotism. I said I have never seen it but maybe it would help.

The next time I came to see her she took me into room with the big comfortable chair. She started doing some stuff and told me that I would not remember what we talked about. Sudden, I was awake, and I looked at my watch and 45 minutes had passed but I thought I was just sleeping. I said I had a good sleep, but did I say anything? She said you talk to me for 45 minutes and answered many questions. I told her what did I say? She said we will discuss this piece by piece but never all at once. I said it cannot be that bad. She said yes it was. I said what? She said you will be able to understand more but we must go slowly because if you are told everything I do not know what you will do.

Over the next few months, I took notes about the dreams and flashbacks and about the discussions I had with the psychologist. I took psychology in college and understood a few things but really did not understand what she really was doing. About five months into our sessions, she finally said I am going to tell you what happened to you when you were six years old. I have no idea why, but I started sweating. She said you must relax and calm down because you are hyper-ventilating. I knew I was in trouble because I did not want her to a talk. For the next 20 minutes she tried to calm me down but for some reason, I felt like I was bad inside. She finally said you have had too much today, and we must just stop here.

I had told the doctor that she may talk to Sheila about anything we do. I later learned that Sheila talked to her after each secession. I went for a few more weeks and finally she said it is time that we talk about just one incident. I said is it really that bad. She said it was unbelievable and tragic. I looked into her eyes and finally said do it. Do you remember your cousin Johnny who was 15 years old when you were 6 years old? I said yes, he used to hurt me a lot. Do you remember him when he had a knife? I said no he never had a knife. Do you remember when he tied your hands and then put the rope over a **bolt so that you were hanging with your feet barely touched the ground.** I said I do not know what you are talking about because that never happened. She went on about me hanging by the rope. Finally, she said close your eyes and look, with your eyes closed, can you see your cousin. I looked with my mind and could see him standing out in front of me. I told her I can see him. She said slowly look at his arm, and now look down at his hand. Suddenly there was the knife. I said nothing but she continued. What happened?

I went for a walk down a path to the big trees. She said look at him what is he doing, does he have his hand in the air with the knife in his hand? I thought my mind was going to blow up. She said stay with me and look at the knife, is it coming at you? Did the knife hit you? Were you cut? How many times were? Did anyone help you? With that I open my eyes looked at her and walked out.

As soon as I got home my wife knew what was going to happen today. I was so tired that I was going to bed. Sheila called the doctor to find what happened. The last paragraphs I wrote took almost four months of terror, and dreams with flashbacks. I just wanted to do my engineering because I wanted to be the best at what I did, and to be a good husband and father.

The pain I have endured both mentally and physically from my youth and the jeep accident is almost more than anyone can withstand. Again, I must stop because it is more than I can stand.

Well, I am back, and it has been three weeks and I cannot look at my note pads. I even stopped going to see my shrink. But now I know I must finish this. Over the next year we worked through many horrors I was subjected to. I will not write about them at this time because I do not have the strength to go through them. Maybe in the future I can write it down. I thank God my Sheila was there, or I probably would be dead.

I have stopped this project more than 100 times because the memories were too painful. Sometimes I would just stare off into space and would look at my notes and just say I cannot do this. But after a couple days I would start again but never go to the worst memories because the pain would suffocate me. Time and time again I tried to think about the worst pain memories, and I would just stop and shake my head, I just could not go there. So, I decided I could write some of the painful memories but never the worst.

Back on patrol I got a radio transmission telling me to go to the artillery headquarters. When I arrived, the first sergeant and five other men were waiting for me. They told me there was a soldier who lost his mind and was babbling and ran off with a big knife. I called the police station and ask for more patrolmen to help me. The patrolmen came and there were five patrolmen along with me, and we started to look for the soldier. We came upon a soldier and ask him if he had seen anybody acting strangely. He told me a man ran at him with a knife but just continued running past him. We found out where the soldier ran so, we went after him.

I told my partner to separate so we could cover more area. I had an idea that the soldier had headed north on the base and was in the trees. After an hour I saw something move so I headed that way. Finally, I found him in a bush still holding his knife. I looked at him and could hardly see him and ask him if he would drop the knife? He said no, take your gun and shoot me. So, I asked him his name. He told me it was Jerry and why do I want to know that. I said Jerry you are a good man tell me what is wrong. He tried to talk but could not, and then he said again kill me I am not worth living. I did have my gun, but it was still in my holster. I made sure there was a bush between us and at least 10 feet so if he came at me, I could have time to get the knife, but I did not want to shoot him.

We talked for 20 minutes and finally I said drop the knife and let us go back. He said nothing and he started to walk towards me. He could not see my hand, but I had pulled out my 45 and took the safety off. As he approached, I thought to myself I am gone to have to shoot him. I told him to drop the knife. But he just kept walking towards me. Finally, I raised my gun, and I moved sideways behind another bush, and he kept coming. I heard a noise behind me, and it was a patrolman. The patrolmen told me he had been watching me about 10 minutes. Finally, I took my club out and threw it at him. The club with 10 ounces of lead hit him in the forehead and he went down. I said Jerry I do not want to hurt you just drop the knife. As he lay there, I hoped he would just drop the 10-inch knife. He started to get up and other patrolmen grabbed the knife in hand and yelled help me. Finally, it was over. Jerry started to weep. We walked him back to the first sergeant and told the first sergeant what you want us to do with him? The first sergeant felt sorry for Jerry and told us he would take care of the situation. I went over to Jerry and told him it is not the end of the world, and you will get better.

We got a new sergeant to our unit. He had been in Vietnam and been shot three different locations and no one knew how bad his PTSD was. They took care of Jerry for two days and then someone escorted him back to the United States to a hospital. I started to walk away and then remembered this is the real cost of war. Shattered live and scars both physical and mental. I honestly believe that Jerry had been shattered and no one could see that he could not function. A few months went by, and I needed to know how Jerry was doing. I called the main hospital he had been sent to and learned his parents and younger sister had come to a hospital and took him home. I hung up the phone and said to my partner I hope he can put it together.

It still amazes me that I worked through the disgusting childhood that I never had. My cousin called me, and she said that Johnny had been knifed in a bar and someone put a 10-inch blade in his belly and in his heart, he was dead before he hit the floor. I thought to myself what goes around comes around. Johnny was only 35 years old, and no one saw the person who stabbed him. I thought it was the whole bar that wanted him gone and they did it. Last night I went to bed at 11:00 PM, and then 3:00 AM woke from a dream about a bear coming up the stairs to my room. I had this dream when I was six years old. This dream which I had many times until my psychologist explained what happened. I was asleep and heard the stairs squeak. I put the covers over my head and hoped it would go away. I knew I was awake but then I heard the floors squeak, and it was getting closer. The room was dark, then my cover started to move, and I could see that the bear was looking at me. I had told the psychologist under hypnosis what had happened. It had been my older brother with a real bear coat on. My father used the coat when he plowed the field in the late fall. I do not know how many times I had the nightmare and now it was just a stupid teenager.

I have been working on my book or what I call a project for over three years and hoping to be done in another six months. When working on my project I remembered the infants that my wife Sheila and I had taking care of seventeen premature infants. A typical baby that we would have would be three or four weeks. It was fun and we always gave them a name. The 9th baby we got was a little boy and weighed in at 3 pounds 2 ounces. We gave him the name of Andrew. At his weight it required feeding about ¾ of an ounce every hour.

Sheila took care of him during the day. I would take care of him during the night. I would hold him in the old rocking chair and would set up 5 bottles on the end table. When he started to fuss and move around, I would give a bottle to him and rock. After he finished his bottle, he would fall asleep, and I would fall asleep with him. All night he would wake up and move which woke me up and we continued this all night. Sheila would not accept money for any of our services. After about a month we started to get attached to the baby. Then another month went by, and we were more attached to him. By the end of three months, we got a call from the state where they had a family who would adopt Andrew. We talked to each other and said I do not think I can do this again. Three months is too long.

Finally, we got a call to go and get our new baby. Sheila had called me that it was time for our first child. I got excited left work we went downtown and kicked out a white fur baby sack with a hood. It was gorgeous and expensive. I was so excited I pulled out of the parking lot and a friend of mine ran out into the street waving both hands. He said you are going down a one way the wrong way. We both startle laughing and I told him that good news about her new daughter. Everybody says this what she was the most beautiful baby.

Nicole would be our first baby and between Sheila and my mother-in-law and I did not get a chance to hold her very much. So I sat on the sideline and smiled. It was great to be a papa. I usually went to work at 4:00 AM so I could get my reports completed when no one was there to bother me. After that I went to see clients and complete engineering projects. I always was home at by 530 pm to be with the family.

All my life I would read books on science. I found a book which tried to define dark matter. The best way to define this work is by example. We said a spaceship into space in the area where the temperature of the earth did not affect samples of what is in outer space. A sample was taken and returned to earth. The sample contained nothing. When in outer space the temperature was 4° Kelvin. Everywhere they went it was 4°. Think about this! There is nothing there, but it has the temperature of 4°everywhere. We will come back to this. Calculations have been made of the milky way which is where earth is located. They found that a force is required to hold all the planets and suns together. In other words, this force is there but we do not know what it is. The force is everywhere. For many years scientists have tried to define and complete testing even with the collider. Now we have a force which is everywhere but cannot figure out what it is made of. If the temperature out there is 4°, the amount of energy to keep space at a constant temperature is huge or infinite.

In the bible it states that God is in us, around us and everywhere. The force we talked about is in us, around us and everywhere. We cannot see it, test for it but we know that it is there. Please think about this!

My wife and I received a letter from governor Janklow where he praised the work and effort that my wife and I had put into new so many premature babies. They were nice to take the time to acknowledge the decent work of people like us. When we started the adopted our son the law stated that the child must be return to the hospital where the child was born. So, when he gets over three pounds, we had to drive too Rapid City, South Dakota which was 350 miles. Where new we were going to get a premature baby with many problems, and we know he was in intensive care, so we went to the Sioux Falls hospitals and saw him. Ryan had to be taken by air ambulance from Sioux Falls to rapid city regional hospital. We had to get in our car and drive 350 miles in a snowstorm. Since we were well versed on premature infants, we stayed at the hospital for one day. We took Ryan to our car with a breathing monitor and a heart monitor and headed for a Sioux Falls. Usually a 6-hour driving time but because of the snow and snow packed rough roads we would be a on the road for more than 13 hours driving time.

After being home with Ryan my wife got mad that the state had spent more than $10,000.00 to fly Ryan from Sioux Falls to Rapid City by an ambulance from Denver Colorado. My wife sat down and composed a letter to governor Janklow. Dear Mr. Janklow, it went. I am glad (sorry) to see money being wasted because we had to get our son 350 miles west when we observed him in a Sioux Falls hospital. But we could not get him in Sioux Falls but had to drive to Rapid City because that was his origin at Berth. The state of South Dakota spent more than $10,000 to complete that journey. We could have drove 4 miles to a hospital in Sioux Falls and picked him up.

In addition, when babies are put up for adoption it can take months for a decision by the mother. We absolutely know how difficult this decision is to make. However, many of the babies are adopted out so that this time for deciding must be minimized both for the mother and for the baby. This decision should not linger for months.

Well within a few months a law was passed where the baby could be placed from any state organization that handles adoption. In addition, that time for the mother's decision was reduced to, I believe, three days. We got a letter from the governor thanking Sheila for her effort to save wasted money and, also to get the babies to their new families as soon as possible. Sheila worried about the three-day limit, so she went to state of South Dakota, Lutheran and Catholic adoption agency and met with many of the young girls to discuss the three-day limit. Out of 24 young girls giving birth only one said she needed more time. Sheila went to this young girl when she was giving birth and the next day wanted to know what her decision at on might be? The young girl started crying so Sheila pulled up a chair took her hand, and both were silent for more than an hour. It was lunchtime so Sheila went out of the hospital and obtained a big juicy burger and fries for the young girl.

Sheila returned the next day because that young girl had no family in the area, and she was alone at 18 years old. I will die in this person Sara but that is not her real name. All day long Sarah was talking with Sheila. Sheila told her that if the baby is given to a mature mother that would be good. Sara had told Sheila she did not have any work and was living in a rundown apartment with her boyfriend. The boyfriend did not want anything to do with the baby.

The boyfriend was only 18 years old and not stable. Sheila went on explaining how she had gotten her daughter and son. Sheila knew it would be hard to watch the baby leave but both would have a better life. The third day came, and Sara decided to adopt the baby out. Sheila stayed with Sara the rest of the day. Sarah had to get ready and go home. Sheila asked her if you want to go home. Sarah told Sheila I have no home either with my parents or my drunken boyfriend. Sheila looked at Sara, but Sara was crying. Sheila told Sara I have a solution do you want to hear it? Sara said why not I have ruined my life. Sheila pulled her tightly into her arms and then both cried for a while.

Sheila had decided that Sara could not go back to where she had been so when the car and drove in it was my wife and Sara. Sarah lived and learned to cook and bake with Sheila. When I got home after Sara was with us for a few months, there was a car in my parking spot. I went in the house and Sara said do you like my car? Sara had gotten a job and was saving all her money to buy a car. Sheila was tired of driving Sara to work. Sheila went to one of her friends and bought a car. She told Sara she could pay her back in the future. I knew what that meant Sara would get the car.

A few more months have passed, and Sara was promoted at the hospital. We knew that she was making rather good money and we would lose her but not completely because she had become my daughter. Sara had become a new person with a positive outlook and a great future. One night we were sitting around with both babies in bed I ask her a very personal question. What do you think of when you found out you were pregnant? By now Sara was confident and understanding of the whole problem. She looked at me and the tear formed in her eye. My boyfriend on a to have an abortion where I did not want to go to that extreme and kill a baby. Did you ever think you might have an abortion? The thought was in my head, but the idea of cutting up a beautiful baby so I would not have a problem was not the solution. I had a decision to wait till it or do I carry it. I know someday a child might look me up and I can tell them that I saved his life from misery. I can tell him that I loved him so much that I cannot keep him.

The main life goal for Sheila was to have a big family and to give me children. Some nights I would wake up and Sheila would be crying. I knew why so I turned over put my arms around her and squeezed. I told her 1000 times I have my two children and they are God's children. We lay there until the sun came out and Sheila was calm and bounced out of bed saying our little angel's heart monitor is going off.

I had a baseball glove and I told Sheila bring Ryan to me. I place Ryan in the glove with his legs curled up I could see leather in the glove all around him. I must get a picture of this. So, Sheila got the camera and film and took a picture. Ryan at birth was only 15 inches long and under 2 pounds. The heart monitor or the breathing monitor would go off from two to 20 times that night. I would jump over the bed and run to his room maybe four steps and ready to do CPR. This went on for more than one year.

I have been working on my book or what I call a project for over two years and hoping to be done in another six months. When working on my project I remembered the fun that my wife Sheila and I had taking care of seventeen premature infants. A typical baby that we would have would be three or four weeks. It was fun and we always gave them a name. The 9th baby we got was a little boy and weighed in at 3 pounds 2 ounces. We gave him the name of Andrew. At his weight it required feeding about ¾ of an ounce every hour.

Sheila took care of him during the day. I would take care of him during the night. I would hold him in the old rocking chair and would set up 5 bottles on the end table. When he started to fuss and move around, I would give a bottle to him and rock. After he finished his bottle, he would fall asleep, and I would fall asleep with him. All night he would wake up and move which woke me up and we continued this all night. Sheila would not except money for any of our services. After about a month we started to get attached to the baby. Then another month went by, and we were more attached to him. By the end of three months, we got a call from the state where they had a family who would adopt Andrew. We talked to each other and said I do not think I can do this again. Three months is too long.

Finally, we got a call to go and get our new baby. Sheila had called me that it was time for our first child. I got excited left work we went downtown and kicked out a white fur baby sack with a hood. It was gorgeous and expensive. I was so excited I pulled out of the parking lot and a friend of mine ran out into the street waving both hands. He said you are going down a one way the wrong way. We both startle laughing and I told him that good news about her new daughter. Everybody says this what she was the most beautiful baby.

Nicole would be our first baby and between Sheila and my mother-in-law and I did not get a chance to hold her very much. So, I sat on the sideline and smiled. It was great be in a papa. I usually went to work at 4:00 AM so I could get my reports completed when no one was there to bother me. After that I went to see clients and complete engineering projects. I always was home at by 530 pm to be with the family.

All my life I would read books on science. I found a book which tried to define dark matter. The best way to define this work is by example. We said a spaceship into space in the area where the temperature of the earth did not affect samples of what is in outer space. A sample was taken and returned to earth. The sample contained nothing. When in outer space the temperature was 4° Kelvin. Everywhere they went it was 4°. Think about this! There is nothing there, but it has the temperature of 4°everywhere. We will come back to this. Calculations have been made of the milky way which is where earth is located. They found that a force is required to hold all the planets and suns together. In other words, this force is there but we do not know what it is. The force is everywhere. For many years scientists have tried to define and complete testing even with the collider. Now we have a force which is everywhere but cannot figure out what it is made of.

If the temperature out there is 4°, the amount of energy to keep space at a constant temperature is huge or infinite.

In the bible it states that God is in us, around us and everywhere. The force we talked about is in us, around us and everywhere. We cannot see it, test for it but we know that it is there. Please think about this!

My wife and I received a letter from Governor Janklow where he praised the work and effort that my wife and I had put into new so many premature babies. They were nice to take the time to acknowledge the good work of people like us. When we started the adopted our son the law stated that the child must be return to the hospital where the child was born. So when he gets over three pounds, we had to drive too Rapid City, South Dakota which was 350 miles. Where new we were going to get a premature baby with many problems, and we know he was in intensive care, so we went to the Sioux Falls hospitals and saw him. Ryan had to be taken by air ambulance from Sioux Falls to Rapid City regional hospital. We had to get in our car and drive 350 miles in a snowstorm. Since we were well versed on premature infants, we stayed at the hospital for one day. We took Ryan to our car with a breathing monitor and a heart monitor and headed for a Sioux Falls. Usually a 6-hour driving time but because of the snow and snow packed rough roads we would be a on the road for more than 13 hours driving time.

After being home with Ryan my wife got mad that the state had spent more than $10,000.00 to fly Ryan from Sioux Falls to Rapid City by an ambulance from Denver Colorado. My wife sat down and composed a letter to Governor Janklow. Dear Mr. Janklow, it went. I am glad (sorry) to see money being wasted because we had to get our son 350 miles west when we observed him in a Sioux Falls hospital. But we could not get him in Sioux Falls but had to drive to Rapid City because that was his origin at Berth. The state of South Dakota spent more than $10,000 to complete that journey. We could have drove 4 miles to a hospital in Sioux Falls and picked him up.

In addition, when babies are put up for adoption it can take months for a decision by the mother. We absolutely know how difficult this decision is to make. However, many of the babies are adopted out so that this time for deciding must be minimized both for the mother and for the baby. This decision should not linger for months.

Well within a few months a law was passed where the baby could be placed from any state organization that handles adoption. In addition, that time for the mother's decision was reduced to, I believe, three days. We got a letter from the governor thanking Sheila for her effort to save wasted money and, also to get the babies to their new families as soon as possible. Sheila worried about the three-day limit, so she went to state of South Dakota, Lutheran and Catholic adoption agency and met with many of the young girls to discuss the three-day limit. Out of 24 young girls giving birth only one said she needed more time. Sheila went to this young girl when she was giving birth and the next day wanted to know what her decision at on might be? The young girl started crying so Sheila pulled up a chair took her hand, and both were silent for more than an hour. It was lunchtime, so Sheila went out of the hospital and obtained a big juicy burger and fries for the young girl.

Sheila returned the next day because that young girl had no family in the area, and she was alone at 18 years old. I will die in this person Sara but that is not her real name. All day long Sarah was talking with Sheila. Sheila told her that if the baby is given to a mature mother that would be good. Sara had told Sheila she did not have any work and was living in a rundown apartment with her boyfriend. The boyfriend did not want anything to do with the baby.

The boyfriend was only 18 years old and not stable. Sheila went on explaining how she had gotten her daughter and son. Sheila knew it would be hard to watch the baby leave but both would have a better life. The third day came, and Sara decided to adopt the baby out. Sheila stayed with Sara the rest of the day. Sarah had to get ready and go home. Sheila asked her if you want to go home. Sarah told Sheila I have no home either with my parents or my drunken boyfriend. Sheila looked at Sara, but Sara was crying. Sheila told Sara I have a solution do you want to hear it? Sara said why not I have ruined my life. Sheila pulled her tightly into her arms and then both cried for a while.

Sheila had decided that Sara could not go back to where she had been so when the car and drove in it was my wife and Sara. Sarah lived and learned to cook and bake with Sheila. When I got home after Sara was with us for a few months, there was a car in my parking spot. I went in the house and Sara said do you like my car? Sara had gotten a job and was saving all her money to buy a car. Sheila was tired of driving Sara to work. Sheila went to one of her friends and bought a car. She told Sara she could pay her back in the future. I knew what that meant Sara would get the car.

A few more months have passed, and Sara was promoted at the hospital. We knew that she was making rather good money and we would lose her but not completely because she had become my daughter. Sara had become a new person with a positive outlook and a great future. One night we were sitting around with both babies in bed I ask her a very personal question. What do you think of when you found out you were pregnant?

By now Sara was confident and understanding of the whole problem. She looked at me and the tear formed in her eye. My boyfriend wanted me to have an abortion where I did not want to go to that extreme and kill a baby. Did you ever think you might have an abortion? The thought was in my head, but the idea of cutting up a beautiful baby so I would not have a problem was not the solution. I know someday a child might look me up and I can tell them that I saved his life from misery. I can tell him that I loved him so much that I could not keep him.

Now, I want to tell you how great the injuries I received when a passenger in the patrol jeep overseas and we were only making a left turn. The person driving the bus that hit us was previously a NAZI and he intended to try and kill us. Read the following letter I sent to the veteran's service because I wanted some services from the VA to help me with pain control and maybe more surgeries to stop the pain. Please read the following:

Michael Ollerich

Union County Veterans Service   March 12, 2019
209 East Main St. Ste 110
Elk Point, SD 57025
Attn: Susan Irons   sirons@lincolncountysd.org
But the
Ref: Sgt Michael J Ollerich

You requested that I write about my time in the army. I am writing about problems I had over 50 years ago so I might make a mistake. I went to basic training in Ft Hood. Then for advance training in Ft Huachuca Az. When I was attached to the 1st armored in Ft Hood Texas. I was running telephone lines so the 8 eight-inch guns would have communication. On the 3rd day I walked by the guns when they fired. I was knocked to the ground. Someone ran over to help me, but I could not hear them. After about a week I could hear some, but my ears would ring all the time. I cannot hear anyone if we are in a group and talking. After a few months I was sent to Germany.

In Germany, I was attached to the 385th MP battalion and spent time in Stuttgart, Crailsheim and Swabbish Hall.

I was riding in a small jeep when I told the driver we were going the wrong way. The jeep driver from Sioux City slowed to about 5 mph and was turning left when a speeding bus (I was told later he was going more than 60 mph. The bus came over a steep hill and hit us. I was thrown out of the jeep and landed about 70 feet into a ditch. I started to come to, but I could not see. My sight came back to a very blurry state. I then looked up and saw what could be an ambulance. The ambulance took about ½ hour to get there. I learned much of this later from the police report. I felt people lifting me up. I was carried to the ambulance. I came to a few days in the hospital. A nurse asked me if I knew where you were. I said it looks like a hospital. She said where and I replied in Sioux Falls SD. She said no Germany. I said why am I here? She said I was in the Army. I said no way. I do not remember anything after that because I passed out. I think I woke the next few days; I do not know.

The jeep has tubing at the front of the seat. My legs were black from my knee to the ankle and 4 inches wide. The Doctor came and said my back had many fractures and bulging discs. A few days later I called my unit to come get me. I told the doctor I would go to my unit and be a desk sergeant. By the time I got to my unit the pain was killing me. I went to the base doctor and said what had happened. He looked me over and my legs and back of my legs were all black. He said if you are in that much pain we need to go back to the hospital. I had brought x-rays and other papers with me and gave them to the Doctor. Based on all the damage you might not walk without crutches. The best thing would be a medical discharge and go to a hospital in the states.

Months went by and I got better but I always had extreme pain, could not run, or walk fast. I could never run or even walk fast. When I got out of the Army, I could walk 50 feet with much pain and then I had to sit down.

I finally could walk and pull patrol. During the time I could not walk I worked on cold cases and settled 6 the first few months. The CID wanted me so they could get recognition, but I said no because I had to sign for another year. Because of the pain and no pain pills I needed out of the army. I did make detective because of this.

I did get better and went to college. In college I got a degree in civil engineering. Working I still had a lot of pain. Then one day brushing my teeth I collapsed on the floor and could not move my legs. The pain was gone for a while. I was taken to the hospital where I was in for some time to figure out what to do with my spine. This has been many years and you must now go to the records and see when all my surgeries took place. I had surgeries at Sioux Valley hospital, now Sanford Hospital, McKennan Hospital now Avera Hospital, Specialty Hospital in Sioux Falls and the hospital in Albuquerque, NM.

I believe I had 11 surgeries on my spine with rods and fusions. I had 2 surgeries on my neck with plates. I needed surgery on my wrist, shoulders, knee, elbow and probably others.

I have gone through many years of pain for 50 years. But I would not give up my Army experience. I was head of 18 MPs completed many investigations and got my honorable discharge. My present condition is that I always have pain. When it exceeds 8 out of 10, I will take a med to reduce the pain. If I do not use the meds, the pain will continue up until I cannot stand the pain. The pain is in my spine, neck, solders, knees, arms, hands, and feet. Some days my neck hurts and I cannot hold up my head.

There is more but this information is enough. I was injured about 50 years ago. I have had a total of 29 surgeries.

Three times in my live, I was asked to talk to young couples about life and death. These three had fallen in love or close to it and found that the girls were pregnant. No one wanted a new life of the baby because they were all too young to care for a baby. I will tell you about one because all these stories are remarkably similar. I got a call at 9:00 pm from a man/boy and said I have aproblem and can you come and have coffee with me. I told Sheila I have a young friend that wants me to come meet him.

I got in my car and headed to be a restaurant. I arrived and went in and sat down. Soon the young man came, and we ordered coffee. Well, what do you want to talk about? He just sat and for 5 minutes and then he looks at me and said I have a huge problem. He finally said my girlfriend is pregnant and she is thinking about having an abortion. I told him that an abortion is forever. He said tell me what you would do. I said it is your decision, but I will tell you what I would do and what I believe. I told him I can only say what I would do but it is still your decision.

I told him I am spiritual and not religious. He told me I am the same. I said not the same. I do read the bible and try to understand what it means. Being spiritual means, I am trying to live my life in a way that God would want me to act and live according to his teachings. Do you believe in God? He told me yes. I said if you believe what would God want you to do. I do not know but we are not old enough and financially able to raise a child. I am sorry but an abortion is murder. The infant is growing and soon will be born. If you have an abortion, you will stop the infant's brain waves, body growth, and the infant's oxygen from the mother. On the other hand, the doctor will come in and cut the infant into pieces. If you get an abortion your problem will stop immediately but you must live with the idea that you killed the infant.

My wife has a few cousins that have had an abortion and they are not doing good mentally. In fact, one of them tried to commit suicide because she had killed another human. If you get the abortion, then expect a lot of depression especially for the mother. So, you see you and your friend must live with what you do forever. We talked on for more than an hour. Finally, I said you have a big decision but for me I would say your answer is to adopt the child to a family who will be the new parents. Most likely you will have the child come back into your life and you must tell them you loved them so much and want to protect them, so we gave you up for adoption to parents mature and wanting a baby. With that I finally said please let the baby live.

Years later I got an invitation to go to all three high school graduations. All three young adults asked me why I was that the graduation? I told them I was friends with their biological parents, and I was invited to see you graduate. I did not have the heart or meanness to tell them that they almost got killed by abortion. Sheila and I walked around, and I would look back at the child and smile. All three couples were probably going to have an abortion. After my talk with the young couples they all decided that abortion is final whereas adoption is love.

Our first child was a girl and I know everybody says they are the most beautiful infant anybody has ever seen. But if you look at the pictures, she was the most beautiful in the world. Now Ryan was another boy with many problems. After he was about six months old, we sat down with a doctor to find out what we could do to help him. He had cerebral palsy that meant he probably would not walk; his hearing was extremely limited, and he did not have good eyesight. Sheila would exercise him 4 hours a day until he was three years old.

A specialized nurse would come to our house for two years to train his body so someday he will be able to walk. When he was four, I got a soccer ball and Ryan came up to kick the ball, but it did not move. His legs were so weak that he can walk but not apply pressure to move the ball. After a few days, the ball started rolling and he got so excited that he did not want to quit. Thanks to soccer he would play for hours and at six I coached the team for Ryan to advance. I was such a good coach that every kid around wanted to be on my team. By the end of our first summer Ryan could play soccer almost as good as any other player.

When Ryan was seven years old, we went to the doctor because he was not growing correctly. The doctor told us he would be a little shorter but could have growth hormones which would take him to his normal height of 6 foot. The doctor went on to say that Ryan would need 15 or 20 surgeries to extend his tendons. I thought about my grandfather who was 5 foot 6 inches tall and had four boys all over 6 feet. My grandfather was tougher than all of them until they were 25 years old. I told everybody that doing that many surgeries for a few inches were not worth it. With that Ryan grew without any surgeries.

I headed to my appointment with my psychologist. When I arrived, she told me that she would like to hypnotize me again to get more answers about my childhood. I still do not believe that I can sit there and talk for almost an hour, answer questions and remember nothing. We went into the room with the big comfortable chair where I sat down and before long, I thought I was asleep. After the session she told me that our next session we would discuss one event when I was seven years old. With that in mind I proceeded to leave her office.

On my next visit we both sat down with a cup of coffee. She would always start the same way, by asking questions to stir my memory. She started by asking me if I remembered the old wooden building with a wood floor and a crawl space one and a half feet deep. I told her that I did remember the old building. Do you remember how to get into the crawl space? I said sure there was a small door in the floor. Did you ever open that door? I said no. Did someone else open the door? I said yes, my cousin Johnny did. Did you look under the floor? Yes. Did you go into the crawl space? I said no. Did someone put you in the crawlspace. I started to sweat and could not believe how terrible I felt. I told her that I wanted to stop.

She told me that she only had a few questions so that we could get through this. She started again, did Johnnie put you into the crawl space? I started sweating more and started to shake. Finally I remember that he bent my arm and shoved me into the hole. Did he shut the door and was it dark? I did not want to answer but finally said yes. Were you scared and could you see? I was scared and I could not see anything. Did you try to open the door? I did not want to go on but answered yes but there was something on it. Did you try to crawl around to find our way out? Yes, I did it for hours but finally I just stopped. How long were you in there? I told her most of the day and I was very hungry. After a few hours I figured that I would die there. But then I was on my path headed for the big trees when suddenly, the door opened but no one was there. Finally, she looked at me and said I think we have accomplished a lot and now we should stop for today.

When I got home my Sheila was there with tears in her eyes because of my doctor had called her and explained what had happened. I was upset and just wanted to be alone, but Sheila said no we are going on a picnic to clear your mind. Sheila was understanding and could always get me to come back and settle down. Sheila had already had a picnic basket and out the door we went. She told me that you would drive because she had a special place by the falls which was our special place.

I was back on patrol and decided to park my patrol car and watch the traffic. I started to think back about high school. When I was just starting high school, everybody was called to the gymnasium. The people called were the freshman boys. One of the priests told us that we would be electing the president for the class. They said we could have 15 minutes to think about it and then we would vote. Everybody starts talking and they said why not vote for me. I could not believe that and with the voting to be determined by the show of hands.

When I got to my new high school I talked to a lot of the boys and was made an honorary north ender. Finally, there were five names on the board. When they said who votes for Mike? The hands went up and I had more than one half of the votes. Therefore, I would be the president. But the priest said we should use ballots just like they do the president of the United States. I told the priest that I was the president already. He said no we are going to do it over. So everybody put their ballot in, and another boy was chosen. I knew that would happen because it was all politics, and the catholic priest would lie. I don't have good opinions of priests. I walked up to the priest and said I want to count the ballots. He said they are in the office, and I do not know if they were thrown away. Now you understand why I quit being a catholic at the age of nine years old.

My brother and I were in the same class and we both liked basketball. Everything in the catholic high school was determined by how much money the family had. When I was a junior, we were on the junior varsity team. In my junior year we did not lose a game and the main school basketball team had lost half of their games. During practice, our coach asked the coach for the A team if we could practice with them. We started the practice and by halftime we were ahead by eight points. You see, the school had selected the A team by how much money their families had and not by their abilities. Now you know why I was not a catholic because they were too dishonest and only look at the family's money.

I continued patrol and found a different place 5 mile up the mountain where the military vehicles could travel fast because the grade down the mountain was 6%. I saw a big truck and trailer going 65 miles per hour. I put on by flashing lights and siren and started to chase them. The speed limit in this area was 35 miles per hour. I finally caught up and read a sign on the trailer with the words "explosives keep 100 yards. I put on the brakes and stopped chasing them. I had their unit and went to their motor pool to see who had signed for the truck and trailer. With that information I wrote a ticket and went by their headquarters and gave it to their captain. The driver would have two go to court and probably would lose his license.

I do like my job, but I wanted to see more of the world, so I put in for Vietnam. About a week later a plainclothes policeman came to me and said why do you want to go to Vietnam? I told him I wanted to see more of the world. He told me that I could not leave the country because of what I controlled in case of war. It would take months to find a replacement. I looked at him and said it looks like I am stuck.

It had been months since my accident in the pain was high. I could not get pain medication because I would get a medical discharge so every time, I wanted to sleep I had to drink two glasses of whiskey and water. Even after I got out of the army, I did the same thing until I met Sheila. Sheila made me go to a doctor and get pain medication.

Well, I just woke up and it is 2:45 AM. My psychologist was correct to say, until I work through this nothing will change. I have started with a few nightmares and have much more to get through. I cannot believe your childhood could control your nightmares for 70 years. Sheila had met the psychiatrist and psychologist for years to get me help. Sheila tried for years but I was a stubborn person and tried to put everything behind me. I suppose I should tell you what my ancestry is. My mother used to say that we had ancestors that came over with the Pilgrims and some of our ancestors met some of these Pilgrims when they arrived. As close as I can figure I am part German, part English, part Russian, and part American Indian, who knows? I have always wanted to find out which tribe my ancestors were part of. All I know is that my one grandfather was the last name of Jenks was accepted by a tribe located in northwest South Dakota. Apparently, he married a woman who was part or full Indian.

It is now 4:00 AM and I started taking notes about what major events in my life took place to help me along the journey of life. According to my psychologist, I have learned a small amount of my past. Later in grade school and high school all I did was go to school and work hard. In the last three years of high school, I took all AP classes but usually went to class three or four days a week. I would ask the teacher for my homework on Monday and Tuesday because I would be driving a semi from after school on Friday to Monday night or Tuesday noon.

One day I was driving in Canada the summer after I had graduated high school. I broke out in a sweat realizing I must drastically change what I am doing, or I would die behind the wheel of those semis. My brother Jim had been drafted by the army, so I decided to join the army. We both went to see the army recruiter. After talking with them we obtained a list of all types of work we could put in for because we were joining for three years. After going through the list, we decided to go into cryptology. I told my brother if we could make it through those schools, we would be working for a general not a lieutenant. I told the recruiter we wanted to leave today. He was shocked and said impossible. I said why? He said to get into cryptology we had to take 4 hours of testing, get plane tickets, a physical and maybe something else. It was 9:00 AM and I told him give us the tests now. Within 2 hours we were done with the test. I told him to get us plane tickets while we got our physicals. He told us the doctor would not be in for two days. I told him I would go to our doctor for the physical. He agreed and when we got back, we had passed the test to get into cryptology.

By 3:00 PM we had everything done and he gave us plane tickets so we could fly out at 11:00 PM. I looked at him and he said I have never seen a one day turn around for two people this fast. So, at 11:00 PM we were on a flight to Denver and then to Fort Bliss, Texas.

The smartest thing I would do was to join the United States Army. I would find out in the army that I had leadership abilities through studying the military code of justice and the other books they told as to read. I asked many soldiers if they read these manuals, and everyone said no. By reading these manuals I would take over my military police unit at 20 years old. After my accident I would solve cold cases and become a detective which usually takes 10 years or more in the army. By always doing more than anybody in our unit I would excel rapidly. The soldiers who did minimal effort went nowhere. By the time I made sergeant I was in the army for less than one and a half years. It usually takes five years to make sergeant.

Without going to the military police school, I had past all the tests in the top 3% of the typical military police school. Even when I and my first sergeant were amazed that anyone without going to a school could score that high. When I was in Fort Hood, 15,000 soldiers took a test, and two people were selected to go to west point. That was the big honor to be selected but I turned it down because anyone going to west point would end up in the army for at least 20 years. I talked to a captain who had went to west point and was still in the army after 12 years. He told me if you go to west point that means your life will be 20-year decision and I knew that I wanted to be a civil engineer not a military engineer.

I didnot make much money in the army but if you get four years of college tuition plus housing allowance that was an excellent way to save money for college. I went to the army because of my older two brothers, had been in the army. My one brother, Bob, was in the Korean war. He tells how he accidentally found himself more than 1 mile behind enemy lines. He covered himself with leaves grass and dirt. He laid there for three days, and he had enemy soldiers within 10 feet. On the third day bombs started falling and the enemy retreated. Not knowing where they were at, he continued not moving until he heard a soldier yelling out is any here? Finally, he yelled back do not shoot I am an American soldier, and he was safe. He would continue as a forward soldier but would not venture as far as his commander told him to go.

Another important lesson that I learned was how to define evil. I would look at the action of people and define if the actions were evil. My definition of evil is whether the action helped a person's improve personal growth spiritually, personal growth or did the action such as a spanking do nothing more than harm the person or child. This action did make the child fearful or make the child look at the parent as a bully. As this behavior starts the child to look at the parent as pain not love and drives the two further apart. If the action continues the child will look at them and try to stay away from them and destroys the child's perception until the child will possibly run.

When I went to the army, I started as a greenhorn that trusted people but soon learn how evil some people were and soon would not trust anyone until I defined their action as good or evil. I was in a small unit and many of the people knew that I oversaw the military police. Some of them would do anything to try and destroy me. One night I was undercover to see if I could find any one person selling drugs. Without thinking I went to the bathroom in a guest house. When I returned, I took a few sips of a beer that I had ordered. After a few sips I started to get sick to my stomach and nauseated. I got up and went out of the building and tried to go home.

Suddenly, the buildings started moving and were hitting me. It was hard but I kept walking to my home. I made it to the bridge and the bridge was trying to throw me into the river. I was so fearful I just sat down. Finally, I looked up and saw one of my military patrolmen. He said what is wrong. I told him that somebody put something into my beer, and I do not know what it was. The patrolmen help me get into the patrol car and took me to the medics. After the medic observed how I was acting, he said they probably put LSD into my drink. He told me to lay down and then he gave me a shot that put me to sleep. When I woke up, I was fine, so I got up and went to my police station. That is when I started not to trust anyone or any situation.

The funniest situation I encountered in basic training was a black boy who was assigned to our unit with a last name of White. The base commander was a general and his last name was White. When the drill sergeant heard his name, he became scared because if the drill sergeant did anything to Private White, he may tell the commander and the drill sergeant could lose his stripes. So, I stayed close to Private White. Private White and I became good friends. After basic training we went to see the first sergeant and find out what our next assignment was.

On the way we passed by our drill sergeant, and he said is white related to the Base Commander of this base? White looked at him, started laughing and said I have never seen him before. The drill sergeant said I did not know but I was not going to take the chance because I am ready to retire. Then we all started to laugh.

I observed kids in the United States made a game out of drinking under the age of 21. If anyone wants to have beer it can be obtained it anytime, they want a party. For over two years I pulled patrol from 8:00 pm to 8:00 AM seven days a week. I did not observe anyone under the age of 21 that drank alcohol and was found to be drunk. In Germany anyone can go to a guest house and buy a small glass of beer over the age of 16 and for anyone under 16 must have an adult with them. In Germany anyone under 21 is taught how to drink responsibly by grandparents or uncles or aunts. There system works were our system fails. To make a law does nothing limit people under 21 to party anytime they want and make it a challenge because of the law. If I pulled patrol in the United States, you would see thousands of kids drinking because they were not taught how to be responsible. The German method works, and the United States fails but the ignorant people are in charge.

I had been totally alone even in the army. After I started college, it bothered me because I saw normal people going through life and enjoying partners or people just having fun, but I was always alone. Finally, I decided to go see my brother Jim and his new apartment on a Friday night. There was a young girl there and I started talking with her and I found that it was a lot of fun just talking. Finally, I ask her to go to the movies. The girl would be my future bride. Sheila. I was learning how to be sociable which I had never done. It was exciting and for the first time I did not want to be alone. After going to the movies, I realized how Sheila was extremely intelligent, beautiful and she was a previous cheerleader. Finally, I realized I might have met my bride. I was learning how to be sociable and kind to this person.

The one area I do not want to go in is in my childhood. The time for older people to stop hurting me is now and forever. A person that would go to the world of big trees to get through the pain has worked part. Now I have suffered almost 70 years with the nightmares and lost sleep. The many nights of sweating and thrashing around in the bed, dreaming, and screaming with fright until I woke. The many nights I was dreaming and sometimes crying when Sheila would wake me and say you are OK, I got you. For the 45 years I was with Sheila, she created my dreams of being a good engineer and starting our company. I will see her in heaven because I know something about heaven. I remember as a young boy traveling into this sky and watching my body lying under the water and my sister coming to get me safe. I am stopping my project for now because the pain was too much for me.

Printed in the United States
by Baker & Taylor Publisher Services